ROGER SESSIONS was born in 1896 and received his education at Harvard and Yale. In his academic career he has taught at Princeton, where he was William Shubael Conant Professor of Music from 1953 to 1965, the University of California at Berkeley, Harvard, and other universities, and since 1965 has been on the faculty of the Juilliard School of Music. He is also the author of *The Musical Experience of Composer, Performer, and Listener* and *Harmonic Practice.*

Questions about Music

Roger Sessions

W · W · NORTON & COMPANY

New York · London

Published simultaneously in Canada by
Penguin Books Canada Ltd,
2801 John Street, Markham, Ontario L3R 1B4.

W. W. Norton & Company, Inc., 500 Fifth Avenue, New York, N.Y. 10110
W. W. Norton & Company Ltd., 37 Great Russell Street, London WC1B 3NU

ISBN 0-393-00571-2

PRINTED IN THE UNITED STATES OF AMERICA

6 7 8 9 0

Foreword

I WISH TO EXPRESS MY WARM GRATITUDE to my alma mater,
Harvard University, first of all for offering me the Charles
Eliot Norton professorship for 1968–1969. I have been very
much aware of both the honor and the challenge involved
in holding a chair that has been identified with so many
illustrious names, including first of all that of the great
humanist and scholar in whose memory the chair was
founded. Such a challenge constitutes also a stimulus; and it
has helped me to organize, to formulate, and to evaluate
many of my basic ideas, conclusions, and convictions regarding music, as these have developed and crystallized during
more than sixty years of intense involvement with music in
all of its phases. For all this, too, and for the opportunity to
give my ideas public utterance, I am deeply grateful.

My thanks are also due those who attended my lectures, on
several occasions braving the rain, ice, and snowdrifts of the
worst winter that the Boston area is said to have endured in
many years. Their attentiveness, and the warmth of their
response both to the lectures themselves, and to tapes of my
own music which I played for them after four of the lectures,
helped to make the experience an especially pleasant one
for me.

This book presents the lectures substantially as they were
delivered. Some minor revisions have been made, first of all
in order to eliminate phrases and passages proper to the
lecture hall but irrelevant in print. A few passages have been

expanded, and the substance of one passage delivered *ad libitum* in the lecture hall has been incorporated into the written text. The Epilogue was not a part of the lectures as delivered, but was added afterwards.

Finally, I wish to thank the Harvard University Press for its much appreciated cooperation, and in particular Mrs. Nancy Clemente of the editorial staff, for her invaluable help in preparing the manuscript for publication.

Roger Sessions

October 12, 1969

Contents

I

Hearing, Knowing, and Understanding Music

IN THIS BOOK I PROPOSE TO examine and discuss some fundamental questions regarding music. Some of these are questions
which have always been discussed, but never resolved. These
I do not expect to resolve, though I would like if possible to
throw some light on them or at least to make some contribu-
tion to their more precise definition. Others have to do more
specifically with our own time, and regarding these I shall
offer at least a definite point of view.

I believe, however, that I should make it clear that I write
as a composer, that is, as a practicing artist, not a scholar or
critic. My reasons for emphasizing this distinction are partly
illustrated by an incident that occurred about fifteen years
ago. Some published lectures of mine had been assailed by a
young reviewer—a music historian who objected to certain
views which I still hold and which will undoubtedly re-echo
at times in the course of this book. The reviewer also wrote
that whatever was good in my book had been expressed better
by a certain lady, a philosopher, who had a short time before
published what I believe was the first of a series of books on
aesthetic problems. I was sufficiently interested to read her
book, and was delighted to find that we did in fact have so
many points of agreement. I was still more pleased, some time
later, to receive a telephone call from her, in which she spoke
enthusiastically of my book and expressed the wish that we
might meet and talk together. In the course of the conversation that resulted, I told her about the review in question. In
comment, she drew the distinction which I have just mentioned, between the way practicing artists, on the one hand,
and philosophers, historians, or aestheticians, on the other,
talk and write about their art, with the strong implication

3

that the latter could often listen with profit to the former, and in fact should do so.

I cannot quote her exact words, but I am, I think, interpreting them quite accurately. What I believe she meant was that to an artist, whose constant and overriding activity and concern is the practical one of shaping his materials in the service of a creative goal, his own experience is what art means to him, and it is of that experience that, directly or by inference, he is always speaking. Whatever ideas he may formulate are to an overwhelming extent the result of experience, not of speculation proceeding from any other basis. That does not mean that he is impervious to ideas from other sources. It does mean, however, that whatever significance these ideas may have for him will be the result of his having, as it were, processed them in the concrete terms of his own artistic activity. He is not, in other words, speaking out of a background of scholarly research or systematic thought, and the kind of precision that these disciplines demand. Always he is speaking essentially of what he himself has learned, through practice. To be sure, artists have their own area, in which the finest precision is the essence and the condition of their achievement. If their product is to have any value, they must work, and must think about their work, in a manner that cannot conceivably be regarded as sloppy. Many an artist, moreover—perhaps every artist—learns to form the habit of occasionally regarding his work on various levels of perspective—whether in order to judge more clearly whether he is achieving a desired effect, whether in order to assure himself of what in a given context must come next, or whether in response to the need or desire to view his work as a whole. He must sometimes, that is to say, get outside of the immediacy of his work, and see it, as it were, from a certain distance. But at such times he is still proceeding from the vantage point of his absorption in the raw substance of what he is doing, and his purposes, either immediate or eventual, regarding it. Whatever he says, therefore, is—or should be—the result of intense artistic conviction, and its basic criteria are those of authenticity and immediacy in terms of experience. These criteria differ in origin and in nature from those proper to the historian or the philosopher or even the theorist. Hence the misunderstandings which sometimes arise. For my part I do not see why the two categories, artist and scholar, need necessarily be incompatible, provided those who have devoted themselves to the one recognize candidly and respect the basic responsibilities of those involved in the other. In the interests of both, both are essential.

To be sure, in practice things are very rarely as clear-cut as I may have seemed to imply. I have never known an artist of real stature whose interests have not ranged far beyond the limits of his own art, of his own time, and of the arts in general. At the same time, the art and music historians and aestheticians for whom I have had the highest respect have invariably been those who have been most clearly and deeply involved with the art with which they are concerned, for itself, and most sensitive to its immanent values. They have been those for whom art—be it music, literature, or visual art—is much more than simply an object of study. The point in question is one of priorities; and these, it seems to me, are very clear-cut indeed.

First of all we may ask ourselves, what does hearing music actually involve? What do we mean by "knowing" a piece of music, and what do we mean by "understanding" it? I am not

5

speaking of "the listener," "the audience," or "the public." As these terms are commonly used today, they have become stereotyped generalizations which belong at best in a quite different frame of reference from that which is relevant here. I am not implying that that frame of reference is not of interest and concern for all of us. But what concerns me here is the means by which music is *grasped,* by all of us, regardless of the nature of our involvement with it. For it must be clear that the very *existence,* the *persistence* throughout the ages, and indeed the *concept* of music presuppose to a considerable degree a common basis of experience on the part of all of those who choose to concern themselves with it. Within our own culture, we take the common basis for granted, and it is against this background that all of our artistic developments— styles, directions, aesthetic revolutions or other changes—take place and acquire whatever significance they may ultimately prove to have. Its limits are those of our cultural horizon, and expand or contract accordingly. In the absence of such a common basis, music could hardly be said to exist; at best, it would become in the bleakest sense of the word a purely private matter.

Today, probably more than ever before, we all of us hear constant challenges being hurled against the music that belongs most clearly to our own time. It has become very nearly a cliché to speak of the "ever-widening gap" between the artist—or at any rate the composer—and "the public"; and who can deny that this phrase contains at least a very palpable element of truth? The use of these categorical terms, however, conceals the fact that this so-called gap is the result of a very great number of different elements, some of which have little or nothing to do with art, or music, as such. It should be noted, too, that in music at least the so-called gap does not involve contemporary music alone. Concert performers have told me on repeated occasions of the difficulties they have encountered in gaining and holding a large public with any but a startlingly limited number of works by even the most revered of the masters. And I myself, from time to time, have had occasion to "defend" the *Hammerklavier* Sonata, the *Diabelli Variations,* a suite by Bach, or one of the many mature but less frequently performed symphonies of Haydn or concertos of Mozart from the onslaughts of some irate member of the lay public who has felt cheated by having "foisted upon him," as he often puts it, such "inferior" works at a concert for which he has paid good money. Nevertheless, these works and many others like them are still performed; they are also available in recordings. Opportunities to hear them are certainly more available than they were, say, fifty years ago. With contemporary music the case is somewhat different. Not only is it more difficult, but it has not behind it the prestige of centuries. Yet it would seem to me at the very least quite probable that the gap, as we call it, consists not in an unbridgeable gulf so much as in an increased time lag between the appearance of an important new work, or composer, or style, and his or its full acceptance by a large section of the musically knowledgeable public. There is still reason to believe that whatever is of real importance gains eventual recognition, even though this recognition sometimes comes very slowly. Needless to say, it does not always come so slowly. I am quite aware that the view is prevalent in some quarters that everything really good necessarily remains unrecognized for a long time— or even, as seems sometimes to be implied, that everything that is unrecognized at first is necessarily good. More popular and possibly less candid is the opposite assumption that whatever is really good is immediately or quickly recognized as such. Both views seem to me quite untenable and misleading. There is, here as elsewhere, simply no rule. Music is to be judged on its merits, however slowly they reveal themselves; any other basis of judgment is an evasion of the issue.

At all events, the gap, however we define it, does exist, and those of us who compose or perform are constantly made aware of it by various questions we are asked, directly or otherwise, from time to time. Such questions are put to us in terms that vary in tone all the way from aggressiveness or even indignation to polite but skeptical curiosity and even, not too rarely, genuine interest. They generally take one of two forms. On the one hand, we are asked (to put it politely) for whom we are writing—are we writing simply for ourselves or possibly for our colleagues, or for what is often called "the general public"? Or, on the other, we are asked (and this time I give the question in a less polite form) why, if we persist in writing music that is so "complicated," so "ugly," and so "unintelligible," we expect any normal person to understand it. This latter question is of course the important one, and it is by no means peculiar to our time. The question of intelligibility, in one form or another characteristic of each age, has been raised repeatedly against composers by their contemporaries since at least as far back as 1600. Before dealing with it, however, it seems appropriate to discuss briefly the first of the two questions, which is, as far as I know, *quite* peculiar to our time. Stated briefly: for whom does the composer write, and whom is he addressing? Most often the question is so put as to imply that there is something shameful in writing only "for"

8

oneself, or "for" a relatively small category of people. This attitude contrasts curiously with the attitudes of former times, in which independence or, as it was so often put, daring to stand alone, or even trying primarily to please oneself, regardless of the opinions of others, was regarded as an honorable mark of integrity in an artist. Times have changed. Music has to a large extent, and from causes with which we are all familiar, become a salable commodity, and, as we should remember, business must, in order to keep its head above water, constantly expand. To do this it must attract the hesitant buyer and cajole the half-hearted or indifferent one. There is no inherent malevolence in this process. On the contrary, it is quite clear that many of those involved in it are troubled by some of its effects and make honest and determined efforts to counteract them. We must regard it, however, as one of the determining facts of life as we know it today, and realize that it is essentially automatic in its workings.

I doubt whether the fundamental attitudes of composers toward their work have changed very much. It is true that pressures exist today which as far as one can tell never existed before, at least to the same degree or with the same force. I would be the last to deny this, or to deny that the pressures are very subtle and the responses to them varied, elusive, and not to be hastily judged. We have no means of comparing either the pressures or the responses with those of other days; we simply do not know, and guesses are always problematical. But the artist of integrity, I am convinced, always creates as he does because it is his overriding imperative to do so. The composer makes his music because music—like Mount Everest—is there and because it involves him deeply. He falls in love with it, if you like, and finds himself possessed by the impulse to put together tones and rhythms and musical patterns of his own. One may say that he does this because he would not otherwise feel that he is really living his life; or one may say that he thinks of his role not as that of an entertainer or that of a demagogue, but rather as that of one who is contributing according to his abilities to something which he, like many others, has learned to regard as one of the world's good things. The standard he follows is that of music itself, seen through the eyes of his vivid personal experience of it, and relation to it; and if one really thinks the question through, he cannot do otherwise. I was in a composition class once in which some of the students used occasionally to present their contributions with the observation—whether coy or rueful I don't know— "I don't really like it, but, etc." Our teacher invariably made the same reply, as just as it was blunt: "If you don't like it, how do you expect me to?" The point could not be stated more truly or more simply.

The chances are that the composer will discover very early that communication is a two-way affair. He will discover it, in any case, sooner or later, and may well insist upon it. He will always find listeners, if only—as will inevitably be the case at the beginning—among those who are closest to him. Depending on the strength of his personality and his musical impulse, he may easily be influenced by them to some degree. But if his musical impulse, together with his resources of personality and character, is strong enough, he will persist in following his own bent until he, as the saying goes, finds his own public, which he can recognize by the fact that it comes to him rather than he to it. This can happen easily and quickly or slowly and gradually. He may find himself swimming either with a current or against it. If he finds himself successfully and happily swimming in either direction (I am talking about success and happiness in the practice of his art, not in the vicissitudes of life outside of it, and I am talking about swimming, not drifting), the chances are overwhelming that that is where he belongs; in other words, it is where his real musical nature and impulse impel him, and not the result of an effort to conform to the tastes either of the company in which he finds himself or of that which he might wish to join.

What I have tried to point out is that the artist's values are not, and cannot be, those of the market. If one must think of him as writing *for* anyone, the answer is, I would think, clear; he is writing for all who love music, and he may reasonably assume that a decent number of these will come to his music in their own good time. He is not writing for "posterity"—certainly a concept that in our day has taken on some very problematical aspects. If he thinks of his work in terms of the future at all, his main preoccupation may very well be to work in such a manner that he himself, say, twenty-five years later, may regard what he has done without blushing.

After all, this means only that his relation to his work is a serious one. In terms of his art, he has something to say, and is concerned with saying it as adequately as possible. Naturally, he is communicating; his whole effort, in terms of technique, is toward articulateness and clarity. But as my greatly esteemed friend the late painter Ben Shahn pointed out so clearly, it is—and I can do no better than quote his words—"the basic intent and responsibility," not "the degree of communicability," that constitute "the value of art to the public." [1]

Let me then pass to the second of the two questions which I

---

[1] Ben Shahn, *The Shape of Content* (Cambridge, Mass.: Harvard University Press, 1957), p. 106.

cited. Simply stated, it reduces itself to the question, in what does hearing, grasping, or apprehending music really consist? Or, to put it a little differently: what is a composer, through his music, demanding of his listener? One of my admired colleagues and friends, the Spanish composer Roberto Gerhard, once put it very briefly and accurately. What the composer requires from his listeners, he wrote, is "a willing ear—the accent being on willing.' " [2] I could not agree more. As I mentioned a little while ago, communication is a two-way affair; it requires, so to speak, a receiving set as well as a sending set. In the case of music, contemporary or otherwise, a "willing ear" supplies us with all we need in the way of receiving equipment. One really has to insist on this point. The practice of supplying bits of instruction, technical and otherwise, as a guide to the "understanding" of a piece of music, which has been so prevalent in the last decades, contributes far more to so-called "sophisticated" palaver than to the real experience of music, and often leads to attitudes that are hopelessly irrelevant. I am reminded of a weird, though I am afraid not wholly untypical conversation that was reported to me recently by a friend of mine who is active and experienced in the theater. The talk was of Rostand's *Cyrano de Bergerac,* to which one of the younger people present—an enthusiastic aspirant in matters also connected with the theater—referred in passing as "one of the classics." My friend, in wide-eyed astonishment, asked the speaker what was meant by the word "classic." He received the following truly classic reply: "A classic is a play in costume and in verse, which one goes to see for the sake of culture." Quite aside from the *bizarrerie* of such a definition, this is certainly not the kind

[2] "The Contemporary Musical Situation," *The Score* (London), no. 16, June 1956, pp. 7ff.

of attitude to the arts which we wish to encourage. This habit of associating what is popularly called "culture" with the rather bitter pill which is sometimes called "education" is altogether too widespread, and it ignores the essential fact that a work of art, on any level whatever, is first and above all something to be enjoyed, savored, and experienced, not a means of social edification or an object of sophisticated appraisal. Most of us, I think, do know this. But perhaps we should be more thoughtful than we sometimes are, in our eagerness to deal with today's problems of mass culture, to keep such priorities clearly in mind.

What the composer asks, what the music demands, then, is a willing ear; and I think we should assume from the outset that a willing ear means not only an ear that is free of prejudice, but an ear that is attentive, curious, and persevering as well. In this respect music certainly presents difficulties which the other arts for the most part do not. Music in its very nature is impermanent; a musical moment passes, and is gone beyond any recall except that of more or less accurate memory or repetition. We have today highly developed means of mechanical reproduction to help us, and they are an invaluable resource. But they do not make it possible, for instance, to play individual passages over slowly or, without considerable distracting manipulation, to play them over and over. Musicians, of course, are obliged to acquire the ability not only to perform music at sight, but also to read it, hearing the sounds accurately in imagination. Most laymen, of course, do not have time to cultivate either of these faculties. Few of them, therefore, have at their disposal the possibility, on which the lovers of literature or of the visual arts can rely, of enjoying their chosen art entirely on their own terms and at their own desired pace—lingering over phrases, contrasts, or other details, referring back or forward, or pausing for rest or contemplation.

In this connection, it is interesting to recall that listening to music, as we know it, is a comparatively recent historical development. This may seem a rather surprising statement in view of the fact that music is composed of sound. The historical facts do not imply that music was supposed to be unheard or that composers did not care how it sounded. But until some three hundred and fifty to four hundred years ago, music was intended for performance in the church, as part of the liturgy and for the glory of God; for performance at public ceremonies, where it was a necessary part of the splendor of the occasion; or for devotees whose enjoyment of it was in singing or playing it, not in merely listening to it. Or else it was simply sung and passed on, as it were, orally, as for instance in the early days of the church. As time went on, church music developed traditional patterns that were codified and set down in the slowly developing musical notation that was available at each given period, but this was done in the interests of establishing and maintaining a liturgical tradition, and what we from our modern standpoint would regard as a very considerable degree of liberty in performance was presumably taken for granted. The same was true, perhaps to an even greater extent, in the case of popular or, as we say, folk music. This was music which was sung, or danced, by the people; it achieved its character through the language and the moods of those who took part in it. Since everyone who chose to do so was entitled to participate in it, it is difficult to imagine that many people were content with what must have seemed to them the lesser experience of merely listening.

I have dwelt on these facts not for their historical interest but because I feel that they have relevance to the question of listening to music as it presents itself to us today. For the music lover of former times was first of all a participant, only occasionally and incidentally a spectator. As the words "amateur" and "dilettante" ("one who loves" and "one who takes delight") originally implied, he had acquired, in a manner that varied in accordance with his social position, the ability to perform, vocally or instrumentally, or often both, as well. As far as we can judge by the music with which he—or she—was furnished, that ability must have been very often considerable. The music of his day was available to him; he was in a position not only to enjoy it, but to explore it at will. His primary and most constant experience of music was an intimate one, gained to an overwhelming degree from the music which he sang or played himself, either alone or as a member of a group.

This state of affairs persisted to some degree even long after public concerts began to be an established practice. Even at a time I myself can remember well, most music lovers were people who "made music" in their homes. Pianos, generally of the upright variety, were familiar objects, and were there not as status symbols but to be played upon, generally by at least one member of each family. It was by no means unusual to see, in a neighbor's house, a pile or a shelfful of printed music including not only, in most cases, a fair amount of second-rate music, but also some of the less difficult classics— Bach, Händel, Haydn, Mozart, Beethoven, Schubert, Mendelssohn, Schumann, Chopin. Virtually always some music of Grieg, possibly some of Tchaikovsky. In more ambitious households one might easily find some early work of Debussy or some other contemporary of the times. Almost always there would be a set of selections from operas, occasionally a vocal score, and very often a volume or two of four-hand or sometimes two-hand arrangements, very likely of what we sometimes call "standard" orchestral works. Occasionally there would be a member of the family who played the violin, or who sang, with a repertoire comparable in scope if not in volume.

These are, of course, childhood memories, though certainly quite accurate ones; and I must make it clear that I do not look upon them with any real feeling of nostalgia. Indeed, the general musical horizon at that time was in many ways much more limited than it is today, and not only because of all the music that has been written since then. It is, however, true that a very large segment of what was the musical public in the earlier years of this century—presumably the largest portion of it—consisted of people who became familiar with music through making it themselves or being in close contact with others who made it. They were accustomed to being on familiar terms with it, to having it in their ears, even to singing it or whistling it on occasion. They absorbed it and experienced it as something not merely to be listened to, but to be taken to themselves, remembered, and lived with on very concrete terms. A public concert, obviously, was an exciting occasion, at which one could hear not only music which was otherwise, for some reason, inaccessible, but also more familiar music performed by experts. But the relevant fact is that most music lovers knew some music very well indeed, as close participants, even on a relatively modest or even very humble level, through the experience of actually making it.

I am not at all implying that the degree of involvement

with music which I have been describing is nonexistent today. What I *am* trying to do is to point out what "understanding" music really consists in, and the kind of path which one must follow if one is really interested in gaining this understanding. I have referred already to the lover of literature and the means of access which he possesses, to its full enjoyment. What do we actually do in enjoying a poem, a novel, or a written drama? In the first place, I think we none of us ever read a word or a sentence without—at the very least barely below the edge of our consciousness—quite involuntarily imagining the actual sounds of the words or sentences. We do this whether we are reading simply for information or for pleasure. Yet if we are really enjoying a work of literature (and I am using the word "enjoy" throughout in its broadest sense), if we are seeking everything that it has to offer, we go a great deal further than this. We hear its phrases, its sentences, its verses, its stanzas, and become more and more aware of its sounds and its rhythms; and as this awareness increases, we interpret these in patterns and cadences dictated by our own imaginations. If we are reading an epic or a novel or a drama, we find ourselves also forming visual images. We create settings and imagine faces, clothes, props, and gestures. We do this virtually without conscious premeditation, although as our awareness acquires a wider and wider span, we may very well make conscious revisions of our previously conceived images. To apply now a musical analogy, what we do is to *perform* the work in imagination. Or, if you like, we recreate it and make it our own.

I suppose it is unnecessary to point out that music, in the final analysis, makes similar demands—similar in degree if not in kind. I will not dwell, at this point, on the differences between the two media; those which are most clearly obvious are quite sufficient for our purposes, and in the last analysis, different media seem to me incommensurable except on a quite superficial level. But all the arts are products of immense human effort, to which, along with many others, men of transcendent genius have contributed the best of their lives; and the result is that they ultimately demand of those who care for them the fullest attention and awareness if we are adequately to receive what they have to convey. From this point of view, the goal must be not so much familiarity or knowledge in the usual sense as awareness: awareness of everything that is there.

So our final question must be: in the light of present-day conditions, how can we gain this awareness of music by listening alone? Essentially, perhaps, I have already indicated the answer; we must listen to music attentively and re-peatedly, absorbing every moment and every detail as best we can, and learn to retain it to the extent that we can take it with us and recall it at will. If we follow this process far enough, we will become more and more aware—even if we cannot put it into words—not merely of the articulative, or structural, elements of music—motifs, phrases, associative patterns, episodes, moments and sections of contrast, climaxes —but of the character and impact which the music conveys through all of these means. Note that I have, all along, used the term "aware." Certainly I do not rule out such verbal information as one may desire. Such verbal information is abundantly available; it can, however, be genuinely relevant or sadly inept. Its usefulness in any given case may nearly always be judged on the basis of whether it enhances one's awareness of what really goes on in a piece of music, or confuses it. One can be sure that it is the *composer,* and to a lesser degree the performer, whose business it is to make sure that one hears what one ought to hear. At any rate it is *awareness,* not knowledge in the sense of information, that determines, on this primary but all-important level, the extent of one's understanding.

Two points seem to me to merit some further discussion. The first is a very practical one. We cannot depend entirely on public performances, obviously. I do not have in mind primarily the cost and the trouble of attending them; and in fact I shall have more to say, in a later chapter, regarding what I consider the enormous importance of "live" performance in one's listening experience. But one cannot choose the program or the occasion, and it may well be that we have to wait for a considerable time, perhaps a matter of years, to hear a live performance of a work in which we have acquired a strong interest. We are therefore obliged to rely on the various channels of mechanical reproduction. Fortunately these have reached a high level of technical quality, which is still rising and which we can assume will continue to rise in the foreseeable future. The opportunities that radio, television, and the various types of recording have made available are enormous, and far outweigh the many and varied dissatisfactions most of us feel with the uses to which they are often put. In the United States particularly, with a few outstanding exceptions, radio programs remain geared to the crassest commercial standards, television programs to what is most spectacular in the sense of "show business." Recording companies often seem to move for the most part with notably deliberate speed in making available recordings of contemporary music. In spite of all this we have more music available to us than ever before, and for the purposes of our present discussion that remains the important fact.

There remain certain other pitfalls, of which only one need concern us, for very brief comment, here. In a certain sense, these media, and especially our record player, make music of all kinds almost too available. We can turn it on and off as we like and listen to it with as much or as little attention as our momentary convenience dictates. It would be entirely unfair to say that this availability fosters superficiality in listening. It does not do that by any means, in spite of the fact that a member of my own generation, to whom such possibilities became available only comparatively late in life, is very likely to feel a distinct though harmless shock of horror and frustration when a Beethoven quartet, or Toscanini's incomparable performance of *Falstaff,* or even perhaps the *Missa Solemnis,* suddenly begins to sound forth at a moment when one is obliged to keep one's mind on other things. What one must always remember is that this is not the way to listen to music with any profit whatever, unless one already knows it intimately and simply wishes to recall it half-subconsciously. I would certainly go no further than that. But it should be obvious that one cannot pretend to even begin to know a piece of music on the basis of anything but repeatedly listening to it with full and undivided attention. This is, after all, the nature of a willing ear.

On the basis of all that I have said, one can outline some of the possible phases experienced in listening to a new, unfamiliar, or difficult piece of music. One's first impression may be a quite negative one; the music may seem opaque, chaotic, crabbed, dissonant; one may be tempted to suspect the composer of a deliberate intent to mislead or baffle, of perversity, incompetence, pure cerebration, or any number of other shortcomings. Actually the chances are reasonably slight that such shortcomings could possibly reveal themselves so quickly, unless to a very experienced professional ear. But if we keep our ears open and willing, and listen attentively, we may easily discern, here and there, moments or passages of which we feel the impact immediately, however fleeting this sensation of contact or recognition may be. One may even tell oneself: "This at least is 'striking'—or 'graceful,' or 'amusing,' even 'moving,' 'beautiful,' or simply 'interesting.'" This means that we have begun to recognize features in the work and to sense its character; and if we are interested or patient enough to pursue the matter further, we will find that these moments will grow longer. The moments of contact are likely to spread—I myself used to think of the process as akin to the expansion of a drop of ink on a blotter. We may become more and more aware of contexts and may also find ourselves beginning to discover additional points of contact—eventually with the piece as a whole. When this last has occurred, and possibly even before, we presumably have opened the way to other contacts of a similar nature—with other works of the composer in question, with works of other composers whose styles present similar problems, and eventually with any music that on first hearing seems strange or baffling to us. By this time we know there may be something worth discovering, and know how to go about the process of finding it. Eventually, if we persist, the music will become familiar to us and will present no more problems to us than does any music with which we are quite familiar.

What has happened is that our ears have not only accustomed themselves to the sounds, but have exercised the

primary and most characteristic function of the musical ear—
that of discovering, through its pursuit of its own satisfaction,
patterns and relationships on an ever-widening scale. Needless to say, it is these patterns and relationships that from a
material point of view constitute the whole of music, that
embody its character and its significance for us. It is our
awareness of them that constitutes the primary essence of
musical understanding and the beginning of our understanding of music in any larger framework, whether that of society,
history, science, or any other focus of human interest.

Let me add a few brief footnotes. First, I have often been
told, mainly by people who are antagonistic to contemporary
music in general: "Well, of course one can *get used* to anything." Of course one can. But one must add, what happens
then? One is, after all, "used" to a great deal of music that one
finds dull, trivial, or even ugly, with quite an area of choice
between types of ugliness. The reader may have noted that in
my description of the process of musical comprehension I
carefully refrained from making either prophecies or predic-
tions. One may certainly find oneself disappointed, in any
number of ways, at any point along the line, and decide that
that particular line is no longer worth pursuing—that one has
learned enough about that particular piece of music to feel
sure that it holds no further interest for one. One may find
that one has become interested in the novelty—and that that
interest vanishes when the piece is no longer new for one.
Life is full of such experiences. Also, there is always the possibility that one may be mistaken—and that also, as the saying
goes, is life.

Finally, the question may be asked: is it not possible that in
any given case the ear can never discover a pattern, because

the pattern is simply not there? To which I would answer, as I believe I already have done by implication, that the ear always discovers some kind of pattern; that is the nature and function of the ear. But, once more, the pattern may be trivial, inconsistent, or even fortuitous; that is indeed the nature of music which is devoid of interest or significance.

Let me end this chapter by quoting something that was said to me after a recent performance of a new symphonic work of mine. The work was beautifully played, and was received with reactions varying from genuine and obvious enthusiasm on the part of a few to bewildered indifference or even occasional hostility on the part of a majority in the audience. After it was all over, the conductor said to me very warmly, "Never forget: the ear is sometimes very slow, the mind is slower, and the heart is sometimes slower still." We composers know that and learn to live with it. But it does not deter us from addressing ourselves with all the resources that we possess to the ear, the mind, and the heart.

II

Talking — and Thinking — about Music

ANYONE WHO is much concerned with music must surely realize that we are today, to an unprecedented extent, surrounded with an enormous quantity of words about music. Words of all kinds, in books, pamphlets, periodicals, concert and opera programs, and newspaper supplements. And of course talk, public and private, in abundance. All of this ranges in character from sales talk, gossip, and popular hermeneutics to the most impenetrable technical gobbledegook. The words that I have just used have, I fear, a slightly derisory flavor; but whatever mockery there is behind them is intended to be reasonably sympathetic in tone. It is really very difficult to talk about music. As Igor Stravinsky observed, "Verbal dialectic is powerless to define musical dialectic in its entirety." [1] This seems to me something of an understatement. By this I do not mean to criticize Stravinsky—in the context in which it appears, the statement could not be improved upon. He was speaking of the verbal indications that a composer uses in the notation of a piece of music, in order to provide the performer with clues to his musical intentions. But his statement still puts into clear terms the proposition on which my discussion is based; and furthermore, in using the word "dialectic," it raises a point which I feel deserves some preliminary mention. The point is that music, like all nonverbal arts and certainly like mathematics and some branches of science, has its own dialectic, which is not that of words at all. I am aware that some philosophers and linguists have disputed, sometimes rather hotly, the possibility of nonverbal thinking. I cannot say how far this is still con-

[1] Igor Stravinsky, *Poetics of Music in the Form of Six Lessons,* trans. Arthur Knodel and Ingolf Dahl (Cambridge, Mass.: Harvard University Press, 1947), p. 123.

27

sidered a disputable philosophical question, though some years ago I had a rather heated argument with a well-known musicologist, who objected to my use of the word "logical" in connection with music. His point seemed to me quite untenable then, as it still does, though I am obviously speaking entirely from my own experience and knowledge of musical processes, creative and otherwise, and not from a theoretical point of view. Anyone interested in the subject of nonverbal thinking may find an exhaustive and well-informed treatment of it, in terms of the controversy itself, in the sixth chapter of *The Psychology of Invention in the Mathematical Field,* by the distinguished French mathematician Jacques Hadamard.[2] The book as a whole is most interesting for the light it throws on what might be called the mechanics of the creative process, whether it be in mathematics or any other field. It is interesting to note that one of the documents Hadamard cites, near the beginning of his book, is a very well-known letter often attributed to Mozart, which I shall discuss briefly in Chapter IV.

Composers, then, and indeed musicians generally think, as obviously they must, in terms of musical material—tones, rhythms, and combinations and patterns thereof—musical material itself, without any intervention of words. Those musicians who are also teachers, and who are constantly in the position of having to explain or criticize procedures, effects, details of execution, or pitfalls, must be constantly faced by the inadequacy of verbalization: the clumsiness, lack of precision, and heavy-handedness inherent in the effort to translate what is conveyed through one medium into the terms of another.

[2] Princeton, N.J., Princeton University Press, 1945, pp. 64–99.

I cannot help feeling that what I am saying of music must be true of the other nonverbal arts as well. In terms of one's own medium, one thinks fast and precisely and without loss of concentration; the use of words nearly always constitutes a long and tortuous by-path, and above all is quite useless in achieving the desired artistic result. Perhaps an example from my own experience may help to make this clear. Many years ago—1930, I think it was—I had come to a point in the piece on which I was working where I needed to introduce a new and contrasting passage. I was working alone in a cottage outside of Florence and was experiencing one of those frustrating moments which probably every artist experiences from time to time: moments when one knows exactly what one wants, but has not yet succeeded in finding its definitive shape. I remember wandering over the Tuscan landscape for the greater part of three days, with my sketch-book, making try after try. At some point during the three days, still obsessed by the musical problem, I had occasion to describe in some detail and in quite specific terms what I was looking for. I did this in the effort to demonstrate to a young skeptic that music was something more than, as he put it, feelings without object, shape, or significance. I think I convinced him, at least in part. But the important thing is that I knew —and simply from following the music as I had conceived and written it up to this point—what must come next, and was able to describe it quite accurately in words. I knew it, that is, in terms of everything except the specific musical pattern itself. The latter came to me a day or two later, complete and definitive, without effort on my part, but only after I had deliberately sought distraction and removed my mind completely from the problem, the concentration, and the tension involved in my efforts to find a solution. When the pattern did come, suddenly and without effort or forethought, as I was walking out onto the street from a darkened theater, there was not a moment's question that it was what I had been seeking. This also is a type of experience, I am sure, with which every composer, and perhaps everyone involved in work of the imagination, must be familiar. For present purposes I would like to point out that at no time in the course of the actual process of composition were words involved. When I undertook to explain to my young literary friend what I had in mind, I had to find words to describe a musical image of which the general shape, but not the specific outline, was already clear to me. In no way, however, did these words help me—nor could they have helped me—to find the precise pattern that I was seeking.

One could hardly find a better illustration of some of the difficulties inherent in talking of music than the experience I have just recounted. I was trying hard to find the proper words with which to describe a sequence of thought that was carried on entirely in the musical medium itself—by which I mean sounds and rhythms, heard, to be sure, in imagination, but nevertheless heard accurately and vividly. Since what I was describing was a consistent chain of accurately imagined sensations, I was able to find the words I needed.

Let us examine some of the expressions that I have used here, not because these phrases are unusual, but because they are common. I spoke of "a musical *idea*," a "musical *image*," and the "general *shape*" and a "specific *outline*." Idea, image, shape, outline: I have looked up the definitions of each of these words in a standard dictionary, and in each case none of the various definitions indicates in any way that the words can be applied to either sound or movement. I chose the words with care, as the best able to express what I had in mind; and I am quite sure that my meaning was clear, certainly to anyone experienced in music. My purpose in dwelling on these very ordinary usages is not to quibble over them, but simply to demonstrate the extent to which we have accustomed ourselves, in speaking of music, to dependence on terms which are essentially metaphorical.

Consider the extent to which the most commonly employed and wholly unchallenged terms which we use in describing music are metaphorically transposed, as it were, from the realm of vision and space to that of sound and time. Take, for instance, the terms "high" and "low" as we apply them to tones. One can not quite call them metaphorical since their meaning, in our culture at least, is both precise and universally accepted. But it would seem very difficult and even perhaps far-fetched if we tried to justify these terms on any rational basis. I think it could perhaps be done, and of course the terms had an origin—presumably not entirely arbitrary—which may possibly be known by musicologists. I myself do not know it. At all events, it is difficult to associate rationally what we call a high note with elevation in either the spatial or the moral sense of the word. The Greeks called what we consider high tones low and our low tones high, for reasons that had nothing to do with the qualities or effects of the tones as such. It is for this reason that I cite this particular case, as indeed it has often been cited. Not only is it interesting in itself, but it shows clearly how essentially arbitrary is at least one of the images that we have borrowed from the realm of space and vision and applied to that of time and hearing.

In a similar manner, we use the word "color" to describe the characteristic and variable tone qualities produced, or capable of being produced, by different instrumental media or by different ways of producing sound within the possibilities of a given medium. We extend it to include the art of combining these different qualities of tone and integrating them into the whole musical pattern. We use the word "color", in other words, in its specifically musical application quite as freely as we use it in connection with visual art, and adapt it along lines that are analogous. But since music is by its very nature a temporal art, not a spatial or a static one, the uses, the problems, and even the function of "color" in the aural sense differ from the respective aspects, and modes of treatment, of color in the visual sense. In music, "colors" can be combined simultaneously, they can be "mixed" in unison; but they may also, and virtually always do, develop and change. Like everything else in music, they are impermanent, and we, so to speak, exploit their impermanence. On this basis we use them, as by analogy they are used in the visual arts, to enhance characterization and underline contrasts; they throw distinctive features into the degree of relief desired by the composer and the performer, thus assuming an important structural role. They are subject to the most delicate modulation, as also to the crassest juxtaposition, and can be applied gently or roughly as the case may demand. If we make the effort to think of the differences in musical style between, say, Wagner and Berlioz, Tchaikovsky and Brahms, or Debussy and Richard Strauss in terms of orchestral sound alone, we will find them as easy to identify, I think, as differences in visual color in works by Turner, Manet, or Matisse.

Yet it should also be clear that the analogy I have just tried to point out is in reality somewhat superficial, and the *differences* between color in the original visual sense and the word "color" as we apply it to music are very real and very important. The musical usage would seem perhaps much more complex in definition, though possibly simpler in application and in effect. I know I am comparing a field in which I have earned some title to competence with another in which I have at best that of an enthusiast. I am, however, familiar with the spectrum and the infinite shadings it contains. The analogous musical spectrum is, like the visual one, a continuum, but it is a continuity of pitch rather than of what we term color. Furthermore, although it has been customary to define "tone-color" in terms of the structure of the overtone series in any given case, I would insist that "color" in music as we actually sense it depends on a great deal more than that. The essential and most characteristic difference in effect between one instrument and another goes far beyond the single, unmodulated tone that the instrument produces. One cannot measure such things, of course, but I myself am convinced that what we experience as color in music derives much more from the properties of the instrument itself than from the specific tone which it produces. Color depends on such matters as the way the tone is attacked and set in motion; the speed with which it develops its full strength; the kind and amount of control that the player can exercise once it has been sounded; the way it is specifically modified by an increase or decrease in loudness or intensity, or by a rise or a fall in pitch; and the degree to which the player can modify one or the other of these elements, including some that I have not mentioned here. It is evident to me that it is such matters as I have just described which constitute the principal basis on which I myself choose my instrumental—or vocal—colors; it is not mainly the "cold tone," in other words, that is the determining element in musical color, but rather what the performer, as directed by the composer, can do with it. The difference in effect, for example, between a staccato in the flute and one in the oboe; or between a forced accent in the strings and one in the brass; or between a cantilena sung by a soprano and one played on a trumpet. I have chosen these examples not entirely at random, but could have chosen many others equally well. What I want to underline as vividly as possible is the essential distinction involved in the use of a single word—in this case the word "color"—to denote both visual and spatial sensations or experiences and those which are auditory and temporal.

"Color," of course, is only one of many terms used to describe music whose original meaning applies to a non-temporal dimension. I could have chosen other terms—we musicians speak of *line,* of *contour,* and generally reserve the term "melody" for a more limited and specific sense. We use the word "texture" and speak of its thickness or transparency. We speak of "brilliance" in describing certain characteristics of style, either of the performer or the composer. And so on.

My purpose in dwelling on the metaphorical nature of those terms is not to raise objections. The terms are in general use, and for the most part have been so for centuries. I myself use them and depend on them as much as does anyone else. Their meanings are, by and large, none the less precise because they are basically metaphoric.

Nevertheless, like—as I suppose—any thoroughly established metaphors, they involve certain pitfalls. Two examples will, I hope, suffice to make my point clear. The first is one I have pointed out on other occasions, and is neither particularly new nor in any sense esoteric. I have always felt that the word "form"—originally a term containing the notion of stability and spatial extension—as applied to music has at times led to or promoted misleading conclusions, pedagogical and otherwise. We speak, for instance, of "the standard forms" or the "classical forms," forgetting what seem to me certain very relevant and indeed determining facts. Let me give one example—that of the "classical form" par excellence —the sonata. We are often told that the sonata form was created and developed by Haydn, Mozart, and Beethoven. Certainly it is hardly deniable that the largest and most complex designs used by these composers grew out of a common basis of expanded technical resources, which were quite new in Haydn's time, and that, as a direct consequence of these expanded resources, these large designs have a great deal in common. Many years ago, in connection with the problem I am now discussing, I asked two of my most gifted and responsible students, both trained in musical scholarship, to find out for me exactly when the term "sonata form" was first used and its rules, as it were, codified. I do not remember any longer the exact date they brought back to me; but it was some year in the 1840's—fifteen to twenty years, that is, after Beethoven's death. Even I was surprised by the lateness of the date, and I took pains to check it with three distinguished musicologists of my acquaintance. Their names were Oliver Strunk, Paul Henry Lang, and Alfred Einstein, and without exception or reservation they confirmed the findings of my students. The point is that the earlier masters, who, as we know, influenced each other, were not following a recognized pattern but rather were giving their music the shape which the scale of their work, in terms of the materials available to them, seemed to demand. I believe this can be fairly well demonstrated, and that only this can account for the great formal variety that their work reveals. A generation later, however, composers had begun to be more interested in the sharply characterized, highly expressive detail. The interest in tight, large-scale cumulative design decreased; but the patterns established by the classic composers were accepted as, in a sense, "standard" and the newer materials were poured into them as into a mold. The result, in spite of differences in tightness of construction or in the appropriateness of the ideas, was a curious uniformity in both the content and the scale of design. The sonatas and symphonies of this period all tended to be approximately the same length and to follow similar procedures, in startling contrast to those of earlier composers, which reveal an endless variety of formal design on all levels. I am oversimplifying, of course, as one inevitably must do if one generalizes. But I think it is fairly clear that toward the middle of the nineteenth century the sonata form, like other "classic forms," tended to become generalized, and that in a sense there developed a tendency to think of musical form itself as something which is imposed on musical ideas rather than as the shape which the ideas themselves dictate, in accordance with the composer's sense of musical design. Thus, if we choose to speak of the "sonata form" today, we may certainly do so. But we should recognize that the standard "sonata form" may still house music that is nevertheless quite without "form" in any real sense whatever. Again, we are sometimes tempted to apply the term "sonata form," very loosely indeed, to works—like certain works of

Schönberg or Bartók or even Webern, for instance—in which the very premises on which the classical form was based have no real equivalent. What we must keep in mind always, and above all, is that what we call musical form is the design that results from the musical impulse itself, a design of a temporal and in no way predetermined nature. Whatever principles govern it must be derived from the impulse generated by, and inherent in, the specific musical idea. It is, in other words, form in *time,* not in space; and in using this and other terms of an implicitly metaphorical nature, we must avoid the confusion which occasionally results from what is essentially the practice of taking the word itself, rather than its specifically musical application, as a point of departure.

I should like to cite briefly another similar, but more radical, instance of the kind of confusion of which I have been speaking. Before doing so I will quote a remark made by Gustav Mahler, which as far as I know has never appeared in print, but which was quoted to me from an exceptionally reliable source. Mahler, accompanied by his wife, was returning from a concert at which Arnold Schönberg's second quartet had received its world premiere. Schönberg was still in his early thirties, but the quartet already embodied characteristics of a style which, a few years back, was to be regarded as revolutionary to a degree virtually unprecedented in musical history. The work was received with typical Viennese intensity, with violent altercations in which the hostile element prevailed. Mahler raised his voice in protest against the hostile demonstrators, and in defense of Schönberg. On the way home Frau Mahler asked him, "But did you really like that piece?" Mahler's reply was that, no, actually he didn't, "but," he then added, "the younger generation is always right." I quote this because the attitude it expresses is essentially my own. Certainly Mahler did not mean to imply that the younger generation is always right in every instance and in every detail. The younger generation, like every other, is full of conflicting views and tendencies. What Mahler was asserting was the sovereign right of the younger generation to its own experiences, its own experiments, and its own interpretations; he was also voicing his faith that out of these experiences would come not merely the shape of the music of the immediate future, but achievements of vital interest and significance. That is a faith that I, too, share; and if I sometimes make remarks of a critical nature I wish them to be taken against the background of that faith, for what they are worth as arguments, and not as a prejudgment of eventual results.

What I have referred to as an instance of confusion is the expressed aim of certain young composers to create a music that has nothing to do with time, but which instead is strictly static in character. One young composer whom I know well, and whose intelligence I respect, even wrote an article, some years ago, proclaiming that the dominant tendency of the following years would be to bring into being a kind of music in which space, not time, was to be the essential medium. I never was quite sure what he meant, and when I asked him to explain he replied that he had already abandoned the idea.

I have, however, heard various works that seem to embody this general idea, and have listened to them with considerable interest. I remember one piece in particular. Its sound quality was striking and novel. Its static quality, however, though also striking, was not quite genuine; there was movement and even development, though to a minimal degree, and I found, wholly without premeditation, that it was the movement and development that held my attention. The latter wavered and finally disappeared as I became more and more aware that the general effect was indeed static, the movement being very slight and on the surface. I cannot help but believe my experience was typical and in the last analysis inevitable. A really static auditory experience is, virtually by definition, one that has no beginning and no end, since an end of the sound means change, and therefore movement. I believe we all would agree that, if we are confronted with a sound that is both unchanging and permanent, we will inevitably, sooner or later, manage to withdraw our attention from it. Or else we will find it intolerable and withdraw physically, at all cost. We will also find that whatever interest the sound itself has for us will disappear, much more rapidly even than one might expect. There is one other possible course of action. We may be resourceful enough to superimpose an imaginative aural pattern on the continuing sound. But in the end it is the latter, even in this case, which will prevail, through the fact that it acts physically on our nervous system, and therefore has a direct and immediate impact that sounds merely imagined, however vividly, can never have.

It should be clear from the discussion above that an art of which the principal medium is sound must be, inevitably, a temporal art—an art, that is, which not only exists in time, but in which time is also an active ingredient. Perhaps a few words of elaboration are needed. Those of us, at least, who listen to music and are used to giving it our full attention can certainly hear, and be aware of, more than one thing at a time. But, as we continue to listen, our ears exercise their coordinating function and unify the various sounds into one single if complex impression. Naturally, I am using the word "ear" not in its specific physiological sense, but in the sense that musicians understand the term. The ear, then, *coordinates* and *simplifies*. If the separate strands to which we listen are to retain their identity for us, they themselves must, so to speak, work to assert that identity—they must, in other words, develop, or, to put it in more general terms, move. Move dynamically by becoming louder or softer, or possibly by assuming a pattern of *alternating* dynamics. Or perhaps move rhythmically, by simple and regular retiteration, which, however, must sooner or later assume a more interesting pattern if it is to hold our attention. Or move in a pattern of changing colors. Or finally, and most drastically, move in pitch—that is to say, melodically. If our attention is to persist, the movement of which I have spoken must assume a pattern, and one which we can eventually apprehend as significant. It seems to me that these statements indicate clearly the basic nature of our apprehension of music, though of course they reach no further than the very beginning of this apprehension. Yet I would also point out that they imply as well the nature of our human apprehension of time itself. Time, we say, passes; and we measure its passing through our awareness of *movement*.

In music, it is of course the *quality* and *character* of movement that counts. And that brings me to my final point. Up to now I have been commenting on certain problems involved in "verbalization" about the raw materials of music. I have deliberately saved certain other problems, which have to do with technical matters, and with aesthetic and historical categories, for later chapters. I believe, however, that there is one other matter, and a rather important one, that needs to be mentioned here. We composers are constantly asked to speak of our own music—to "explain" it, so to speak. This is a real demand that we face constantly. Whenever a new work is performed, we are asked to write notes on it. We are asked to write what are called "liner notes" for the back of record jackets; and we are often asked to take part in that bizarre ceremony known as the panel discussion. I am not complaining about all this. It is a challenge, and meeting challenges is exhilarating, even when, as sometimes happens, the challenge is not entirely to the point.

What I find depressing, however—and very difficult to deal with—is that it has become a very prevalent custom to offer so-called "explanations" of music in terms of purely technical analysis. I find it depressing partly for what might be a very personal reason; for myself, I can imagine no duller, and certainly no more laborious, reading than someone else's technical analysis of a piece of music. More important, however, by far is that analysis or discussion may tell us something about how a piece of music has been put together (I have to add that unfortunately it can sometimes be quite misleading even on that score). Yet it tells us little or nothing about the character or the intent of the music itself. There are several reasons why this practice has become so widespread. In the first place, there is the kind of confusion to which I referred in the first chapter, which may be summed up in the equation "Culture = learning = information," the more esoteric the better. Another reason is, of course, what has been loosely called the scientific temper of our age, and what would seem to me a slightly perverse attempt to apply principles of logical positivism to the arts, where in my opinion they have no real place. I think, however, that as far as composers are concerned the reason is that the essence of what we have to say is in the music itself and we feel powerless to translate it into any other terms. There are plenty of anecdotes about the great composers of the past which illustrate this point very clearly. Today, since we composers are obliged to talk, some of us fall back on describing what we have done with the twelve-tone row, or how we have exploited this or that technical device, or how ingeniously we have solved this or that formal problem. Such talk would be quite harmless if it did not come "from the horse's mouth," whence it promotes the idea that these matters are what music is "all about." That idea, too, is unfortunately very widespread, despite its manifest erroneousness. Music is, assuredly, design in tones, or, if you prefer, in sound. This I think needs a little further elaboration; and if I may be allowed to hazard what will sound suspiciously like an unsatisfactory attempt to define music itself, I would say rather that music is controlled movement of sound in time. This definition, however, omits an essential point, which is today customarily ignored at least in circles that consider themselves sophisticated. It is ignored partly because we, as late as my own generation, were overfed with the hermeneutics that became so popular in the nineteenth century and that described music in terms of emotion and association—a practice which led to, among other things, exaggerated and distorted styles of performance, tear-jerking vulgarities, and far-fetched interpretations, so-called, of a *literary, anecdotal,* or even, as has become standard practice in the Soviet Union today, *political* nature. In reaction against this we have tended to wrap ourselves in a mantle of reticence regarding what is the central fact of all: the fact that music is made by human beings, who want it, enjoy it, and even love it. We all regard it as one of those things which make life worth living and which in that sense are available to, and in one way or another, enjoyed by virtually everyone. The vogue of scientific and quasi-scientific habits of thought has fostered the tendency to forget or ignore this.

Music is design and controlled movement and time, of which we retain our awareness through movement—movement in action, in imagination, in the vital processes of the human organism, body and mind. We become aware of movement with our first breath and *remain* aware of it, on some level of our existence, until our last one. We begin to become aware of sound, I am told, by making it ourselves, very shortly after we have appeared on the scene. I have to accept this on hearsay, since at the only birth at which I have been personally present I was both too involved and too inexperienced to observe; but the fact is, I believe, an accepted one. Since these are our earliest experiences and since they continue through life, we become very sensitive to both movement and sound, and develop this sensitivity more and more as life continues. Both accumulate meanings for us.

So—beginning once more with our definition of music as "design" or "controlled movement"—we are perhaps entitled to ask "why this specific movement?" "why this specific sound?" I cannot give any very precise answers to these questions, but perhaps I can suggest lines along which the answers might be at least approached.

Let us start from the premise that we are seeking not to discover what music expresses, but to refine our notion of what it *is*. As I have already pointed out, communication is a two-way affair; and if this is so, it follows that what music *expresses* is to a large extent the affair of the listener. I am convinced that music does not in any real sense express *emotion*. Emotion is, in any recognizable sense, bound up with objects, which music does not provide. It would be tempting at this point to say that music is a human gesture; this comes near the point, but it leaves some annoying loopholes. We react, I think, to some patterns of tone that are the product of no human gesture at all or that are not even human in origin. Our reactions are minute and without significance in this context, but they disturb me a little nevertheless. They still demonstrate the immense power that sound and movement exert, and give us an indication of the locus of music's power and of its area of precision. This power is beneath the realm of emotion, in the sphere of movement itself, and the vital significance of movement for us. Let me attempt a few very crude illustrations. Music cannot express fear, which is certainly an authentic emotion. But its movement, in tones, accents, and rhythmic design, can be restless, sharply agitated, violent, and even suspenseful. Music cannot express love, but its movement can be gentle, tempestuous, quiet, and insistent, with an inexhaustible variety of nuance. It cannot express joy or exultation, but its movement can be decisive and fast; it can accelerate, its register can be high, its range wide and its texture compact. It cannot express despair, but it can move slowly, in a prevailingly downward direction; its texture can become heavy and, as we are wont to say, dark—or it can vanish entirely.

And so on. These examples are quite elementary, of course, and I was using words—a very clumsy medium—to describe sounds only vaguely imagined. But musical movement is virtually endless in its variety of range and nuance, virtually unlimited in its range of flexibility, from the utmost rigidity to the swiftest change. Musical texture can be impenetrably thick, or it can assume, at a moment's notice, the tenuousness of a note in the highest register of the violin—produced by a very taut string little more than an inch long. I see no need to go into further particulars, though it would be possible to do so. What music conveys to us—and let it be emphasized, this is the *nature of the medium itself,* not the consciously formulated purpose of the composer—is the nature of our existence, as embodied in the movement that constitutes our innermost life: those inner gestures that lie behind not only our emotions, but our every impulse and action, which are in turn set in motion by these, and which in turn determine the ultimate character of life itself. Music is perhaps the only one of the arts that moves, at least so exclusively, on this level. I do not mean to claim for it any status of ascendancy, or inferiority, for this reason. Every art has its particular realm where it holds paramount sway, and all have grown out of human impulses, desires, and needs. I find Dante and Shakespeare, Titian and Rembrandt and Michelangelo quite as great as Johann Sebastian Bach, Mozart, Haydn, and Beethoven, and not measurably greater. But music is supreme in its own realm, and it is from this realm that it derives its immense and legendary power, to which men and women have testified and which sometimes they have even feared, from the time of the earliest memories that we as human beings possess.

III

Performing Music

A FEW YEARS AGO a friend of mine, one of the leading performers of what might be called the "middle generation," remarked to me that "performers are the real critics of music." This remark struck a sympathetic chord in my mind, since I had for some time thought along similar lines, though not in quite the same context as that which prompted my friend's remark. If I understood him correctly, he was thinking of the critic mainly in the role of arbiter, while I was thinking more specifically of an analogy with the literary critic, who seems to me at his best and most interesting as an *interpreter* of literature, and only secondarily interesting as a *judge* of literature. Actually this seems to me the case with all critics. Understanding must come before judgment, which is in fact irrelevant without it, and incidental with it, and which is perhaps on the whole its least interesting by-product. The point I find relevant here, however, is that the literary critic is using words, verbalized ideas, and verbal images to describe and discuss works of art whose medium is verbal; while the musical critic, as we generally understand the term, is using words to deal with a medium with which words, as I pointed out in the previous chapter, are ultimately incommensurable. The performer, on the other hand, is communicating in musical terms, with, it may be assumed, constant awareness of, and direct contact with, the musical stuff itself—its flow, its successive events, and the relation of these to the total musical design. He is grappling with the problems and demands that the music poses, and interpreting these in terms of musical sound and movement.

I am not implying, nor do I intend to imply, that verbal comment on music is necessarily valueless. Also it must be pointed out that one does not—or at any rate should not—

49

evaluate significant achievement in terms, least of all implicitly exclusive ones, of the position or even the status of its author. A good critic is obviously a good critic, and a bad one a bad one, whoever he may be and whatever his professional or nonprofessional credentials. Furthermore, there have always been, at least since the origins of the written word, verbal discussions of music and its mysteries, of all degrees of enlightenment and interest; and certainly some of the most brilliant and illuminating of these have come from artists themselves, who have sometimes seen fit to discuss their art and occasionally their fellow artists in writing and in print. A very distinguished critic of visual art once said to me, "The creative artist is the best critic of all, provided he takes the trouble." Of course, for one reason or another, he often does *not* take the trouble, which is considerable and in no way obligatory to the creative artist, whose first duty—and last—is to his own ideas. At any rate the artist's inevitable absorption in his own work has led to a frequently heard dictum that creative artists are necessarily bad critics. This is not, obviously, necessarily true. A creative artist may well feel quite secure in the conviction that he can make the works that are his own better than can anyone else, and thus feel free to appreciate the work of others, on *their* own terms. One must remember, too, that a good critic is not by any means necessarily one who is always right—after all, who is, or could reasonably expect to be, since we all of us are expected to develop and therefore change, and should feel obliged to be honest about it?

However, my purpose here is not to discuss critics or criticism, but simply to draw attention to what seems to me the primary and most important function of the performer. It is he—or she—who brings the music to audible life, who transmits the composer's musical vision to the listener. Let me recall the fact, to which I have already referred, that until about three and a half centuries ago the listener as we know him today can scarcely be said to have existed. Those who loved music sang it or played it, and composers wrote their music to be performed, not to be listened to. I think that in the last analysis composers have not really changed in this regard. In those former times, composers were quite as concerned with the way their music sounded as they are today. If one has even a little knowledge of the music of the Renaissance, one becomes very conscious of strong and pronounced individualities, in this respect as in others. Today, the composer is also, and preeminently, concerned with the way his music will sound, and, moreover, he is always fully aware that it is the performer who will bring his imagined sounds to life; and to the extent that he is really possessed by his work it is to this region—not that of the performer as such, of course, but to that of the *performance*—or, in other words, the realization—of his music that his concerns are directed. His concern, as far as it applies to the listener, will be that what the latter will hear shall be that which he has intended.

This seems to be so obvious as to scarcely need pointing out, though perhaps it does need stating in these specific terms. What is less obvious, though, I am convinced, quite elementary, is that the performer is an absolutely essential element in the musical picture. I think it worthwhile to discuss this question at some length, as it is by no means always understood clearly. I myself, in fact, was well on the way toward middle life before I understood it. I remember very well one day, in the early 1940's, propounding to one of my younger colleagues an idea which I was entertaining at the time, namely that composers might one day be able to develop a technique of incising their music on wax records in such a way that their music, complete and definitive in performance, with all the subtlest details of shading and tempo as desired by the composer, might be preserved in frozen perpetuity from the hazards of poor performance, which are, after all, very considerable. It seemed a beautiful idea, but in entertaining it and developing it I was completely ignoring or misinterpreting certain previous and vivid experiences of my own. I was forgetting the day, some fifteen years previously, when I had hurled a gramophone record across the room in a fury, intentionally shattering it. I did this not because it was a bad recording or a bad performance or even a bad piece. It was none of these things; it was Debussy's *Fêtes,* beautifully played by, I think, the Philadelphia Orchestra. I loved the piece, and still love it. But what infuriated me was my fully-developed awareness of having heard exactly the same sounds, exactly the same nuances, both of tempo and dynamics, the same accents, down to the minutest detail, so many times that I knew exactly—and I emphasize *exactly,* to the last instant—what was coming next. The performance of the music had become, as regards my awareness of it, completely mechanical, and I had reacted as one does to any sensation of mechanical repetition.

Or, in connection once more with my dreams of authoritatively and unalterably incised music, I might perhaps have remembered an analogous experience in the visual realm. The occasion was my re-viewing of a film that I had enjoyed and seen repeatedly some twenty years earlier. A silent film exceptionally well acted and produced, by any standards. I found myself laughing at a scene that I had formerly always found quite touching—in which the young heroine, who was shortly to suffer a fate worse than death, with death itself thrown into the bargain, presented a final picture of graceful and innocent gaiety. I laughed not because of any awkwardness or incongruity in the execution—the scene was really beautifully done—or because I "knew the story." What prompted my sense of the ridiculous was a total sensation of having seen it all before, down to the last millimeter in the length, and instant in the timing, of the girl's smile, to the exact bend of her knees, the minutest wrinkle of her skirt or fringe of her petticoat as she curtsied—I laughed simply because, since I recognized in advance every nuance and every gesture, the whole business had become literally "stage business" for me, and suddenly struck me as ludicrous.

I can remember only once having had a similar experience at a so-called "live performance"—at a cabaret in Berlin, early in 1933, where I happened to go twice to the same show. At one point in the show there was a clever three-word punch line, which, however, depended for its effect very much on the timing and mode of delivery. For that reason, no doubt, it had been very carefully rehearsed, and came off beautifully. But the second time, for me, it fell completely flat and seemed completely stale, because I recognized every gesture of the performer and the pitch and tone of his voice in its every nuance. To be sure, this was a very short moment—three words, containing seven syllables; but it was the very perfection of the performance that caused me to remember it so vividly and that thereby completely destroyed its effectiveness for me the second time that I witnessed it.

The experience I have just recounted must seem very ordinary to the reader, who no doubt has had similar ones himself. Such experiences, I think, tell us something about our reaction to experiences that take place in the realm of time. Perhaps I might briefly refer here to the experience known as *déjà vu,* the sensation that one can have of repeating an experience in every respect identical with one that one has had before. A startling and generally rather eerie sensation, no doubt. But obviously no such emotional content is, or can be, attached to an experience of which we can foresee every moment and every nuance in advance, thus remaining aware of the process by which these effects are produced. We may, of course, still admire—and here I am thinking specifically of musical performance—the skill with which it is executed. But, having thoroughly and completely absorbed it, we lose our interest in its repetition. As far as I can tell—and I have pondered this question very much—we can even enjoy the vivid memory of the most felicitous moments of a performance without any discernible desire to literally hear it again. I myself have many extremely vivid and exact memories of musical performance, sometimes from many years back, and have often referred to them, both in thought and in conversation, during all the intervening years. But when I think of the possibility of repeating them, I always find myself rejecting the idea of living again through exactly the same experience in terms of sound—or movement; "I have heard that already," as the saying goes. But I am always ready to hear the same piece, equally well, or better, played, and ready and eager of course to react with the same intensity if the performance is such to allow me to do this. Sometimes this occurs. I heard a performance, less than two years ago, of

Schubert's Unfinished Symphony—scarcely an unfamiliar piece—which held me quite spellbound, as it did most of those who heard it. I remember it with the keenest pleasure; and my pleasure was not only in the inexhaustible freshness of the piece itself, but in the freshness also of the conductor's and, through his communication, the orchestra's performance. I was able to hear anew this symphony, which I have both physically and in imagination heard over and over again since I first heard it fifty-seven years ago, and to find its impact undiminished. This performance enabled me to experience the piece afresh.

I have already referred to the fact that I regard such experiences as typical in the dimensions of *time*. It seems to me that one can make the point in these terms for several reasons. The crucial fact is that in music time is subject to more incessant and complete control than is the case in any other artistic medium. It is true that the dance, the theater, poetry, and prose literature are also, to a very considerable degree, temporal arts. I have tried to list them—very roughly, of course—in order, in accordance with the degree to which *time* is an important factor in each and therefore a factor under the relatively strict control of the original creator. Of all the arts I have mentioned, the closest to music in this respect, obviously it seems to me, is the dance. But the dance is an art of movement in space as well as in time; and the spatial element must constantly and inevitably, by its sheer presence, condition and define the purely temporal one. In the case of the theater, the sheer physical complexity of the medium is still more evident. Everyone who has had any experience in the theater is fully aware of the crucial importance of the element of "timing"; yet he must be aware, too, that effective timing is dependent on a very considerable number of factors that are, in their very essence, variable. My point here is perhaps thrown into the boldest possible relief by the comparison of the spoken drama with opera, in which the tempo, the intonation, and the inflection of the actor's various utterances are subjected, through the demands of the music, to the minutest control, as is the timing of the action itself. The design of the production must be, therefore, subject to the musical design created by the composer; and thus, one must say, woe unto the director who ignores or violates the composer's intentions! However, one must also say, and with equal fervor: woe unto the composer who does not clearly visualize his characters down to the last word and the last relevant gesture, who does not conceive of every moment of the action in terms of its relative weight or emphasis—who, in other words, allows either of the two media, music or drama, to become a mere excuse for the other. Each must play its full role. But it should hardly be necessary to point out that it is on the composer, the maker of the music, that lies the responsibility of timing, in the precisest of terms—and it is the responsibility of the director, in this particular context, to plan his production in terms of the requirements of the music, to the smallest detail within the limits of the possible.

With all of this in view, it is now perhaps possible to compare our ordinary experience of the one art that is most purely temporal, music, with the arts that are most preeminently spatial, in the nonmobile sense. I am leaving out of account what at this point and in this connection one may call exceptional and accessory uses of the one dimension in connection with the predominant other one. I fail to see how they affect the general picture at all. Thus Alexander Calder,

whom I admire and whose work has often given me genuine
delight, has introduced movement into a medium which
nevertheless remains overwhelmingly spatial in its impact.
Thus also, since the sixteenth century at the very latest, composers have on occasion made use of the spatial dimension,
for various purposes. They have utilized, that is to say, the
device of placing their performers in such a way that
the sound comes from different directions or distances, for
a variety of reasons and in a variety of designs. But neither
of these cases alters the essential nature of the situation. They
are, I think, cases of a medium that in terms of one dimension
is extremely *specific,* minutely designed and therefore controlled, and in the other *generalized*—that is to say, either
essentially uncontrolled, or controlled according to the demands of the medium which prevails.

It is fairly obvious, I suppose, that our total awareness of
movement—which in essence signifies our awareness of *time
as a process*—demands sustained attention, which is limited to
the duration of the specific act of movement in question; it
holds us captive, as it were, for the duration. We are aware of
a beginning and an end. In respect to space on the other hand,
the words "beginning" and "end" have an essentially metaphorical meaning; they represent boundaries or limits that
remain even after we have become aware of them, as does all
that lies between. Our attention is our own to husband and
deploy as we wish. We can withdraw it and absent ourselves
merely by averting or closing our eyes, and return whenever
and for as long as we wish.

What I am saying is that we experience music as a pattern
of movement, as a gesture; and that a gesture gradually loses
its meaning for us insofar as we become aware of having

witnessed it, in its total identity, before. If it is to retain this meaning in its full force, it must be on each occasion reinvested with fresh energy. Otherwise we experience it, to an increasing degree, as static; its impact, as movement, diminishes, and in the end we cease to experience it as movement at all. Its essentially static nature has imposed itself on our awareness.

This is why I am convinced that the performer is an essential element in the whole musical picture. It is why I came to realize that my earlier dreams—that composers might learn to freeze their own performances, in wax or otherwise (tape recorders had not been invented at that time)—were, to put it bluntly, quite ill-directed. They were ill-directed, above all, for the reasons I have been outlining; a gesture needs constant renewal if it is to retain its force on subsequent repetitions. Composers above all should know this, especially if they have developed the practice of taking part in performances of their own work. Each performance is a new one, and the work is always studied and approached anew, even by the composer. The same, it should be obvious, is true of professional performers. I would go even much further and point out that there is no such thing as a "definitive" performance of any work whatever. This is true even of performances by the composer himself, in spite of the fact that recordings of his performances of his own work should be made and preserved, for a number of quite obvious reasons.

The legend of the "definitive performance" has grown up with the prevalence and wide distribution of recordings, and with a particular though very familiar form of snobbery that has resulted from this. As we all know very well, devotees of recordings sometimes form the habit of attaching themselves to, and even sometimes of identifying the work itself with, a particular recording by their favorite conductor, group, or soloist. Perhaps it is not now quite so necessary to point out the absurdity of this practice as it was, say, twenty-five years ago. There are today so many different recordings available, of many well-known works, that it is quite likely that record collectors have learned that the matter is not that simple. It may even be surmised that an appreciable proportion of the record-listening public has discovered what I have been trying to point out—namely, that one cannot keep on listening to the same mechanically registered performance without becoming aware, and eventually tiring, of the same nuances, the same gestures, mechanically repeated over and over again. Furthermore, there are certain built-in hazards involved in the recording process itself. For one thing, it inevitably puts an exaggerated premium on total accuracy. In a live performance, an occasional wrong or sour note is to be avoided if possible, of course; but it passes, and is immediately forgotten if the performance as a whole is reasonably satisfactory; if the total performance is not satisfactory, it is certainly not the presence of one or even several defective tones that makes it so. In a recording a bad note is, for obvious reasons, a disaster. It will be heard repeatedly, and the listener may very quickly find it virtually intolerable. Thus players participating in a recording session, intent on exactness, may easily become so tense that they sacrifice some of the vitality of the performance as a whole to their preoccupation with total accuracy. The performance may also have to be repeated again and again in order to insure flawless execution; and since that is frequently not forthcoming on any single reading, the ultimate recording may well be one which has been patched up with splicings taken from other tapes than the main one on which the recording is based. The result is, of course, a loss, frequently very minute and scarcely noticeable, but nonetheless real, of impulse and vitality.

I do not mean to belittle the enormous importance of recordings, still less do I imply that all performances are equally good, or even generally so. Let me consider each of these points briefly. About the latter especially, many volumes could be, and as a matter of fact have been, written. As for the first point, recordings as we now know them—even the best of them—have certain built-in defects of which most of us are quite aware. The dynamic range is much reduced, with a consequent attenuation of contrast; the upper and lower registers are frequently inadequate, and there is a definite lessening of transparency, owing to surface noises and perhaps some other acoustical factors. But these are technical matters that will doubtless continue to improve, as they have done in the past. The part that recordings play in practically every branch of musical life is incalculable, and hardly to be particularized in detail. Moreover, in matters of this sort, sophistication develops of itself, and often tends to confound those who jump to too early conclusions. I have often wished that, instead of issuing quite highly priced, specially prepared and, so to speak, chromium-plated recordings by star performers, the recording business could have developed on a basis of recording—presumably more cheaply—*specific occasions,* and many of them; and that one might therefore buy, at a presumably lower price than that which prevails under present circumstances, recordings of specific performances given on specific dates. Of course I understand many reasons why this did not, and could not, come about—it is not in the nature of either contemporary business practice or contemporary social structure that it should do so.

In any case, I come back to my main point, that we experience music as movement and gesture, and that movement and gesture, if they are to retain their power for us, have to be constantly reinvested with fresh energy. I would like to pursue this point a little further and point out that our sense of energy in a gesture does not derive from a conscious effort on the part of the performer to introduce changes for the sake of variety. This procedure only achieves a result that is contrived, artificial, hence stiff and unreal. A sense of energy, on the contrary, comes from the fact that the energy is really and unavoidably fresh, from beginning to end. It is the result of a real impulse, not a mechanically executed routine. One must emphasize that a real gesture is in its very nature organic. It takes its precise and characteristic shape by virtue of its own energy, its own inherent laws, its goals, its own curve and direction. There is nothing whatever fortuitous about it. Every moment conditions the one that follows, and the whole is conditioned by the original and sustained kinetic impulse. This, in the very simplest of terms, may be taken as what good musical performance consists in—the appropriate musical gesture, boldly, decisively, and, of course, accurately delivered. If the gesture is genuinely bold and genuinely decisive—by which I mean direct and unimpeded *in terms of the desired musical effect,* the fresh energy will necessarily be there; the gesture cannot, after all, be made without it.

All of my observations on the subject of performance should make it clear that I disagree entirely, and fundamentally, with certain devotees of the electronic musical medium, who have at one time or another expressed the opinion that their medium will in due time supersede the performer. Unless I am quite mistaken, this point of view is far less prevalent than it was some years ago. At no time, however, have I felt that such considerations as I have raised implied any logical basis for rejecting the electronic medium as such. The latter is still in its infancy, but it has aroused the enthusiasm and stimulated the imagination of many highly gifted young musicians and will no doubt continue to do so. It is true that, of the electronically produced music I have heard up to this time, that which has impressed me the most has nearly—perhaps not quite—always been associated with "live" instruments or voices. I see no reason to believe that this need always be the case. But I do feel that in its present state of development the medium poses certain very important problems, one of which is that of the diminishing returns yielded by the mechanical reproduction of movement. I have discussed this and other problems on quite a number of occasions with some of the leading devotees—both American and European—of the electronic medium, and have found not only that the problems themselves are now widely recognized, but also that much energy and research is being presently devoted to solving them. Obviously in the case of the indispensability of the performer the solution can only lie in the devising of an adequate and responsive instrument on which music created for the electronic medium can be actually and spontaneously performed. Serious efforts have been made in a number of different quarters to develop such instruments, and no doubt these will ultimately meet with full and unqualified success. I cannot take any stock in the arguments sometimes adduced in opposition to the medium as such—namely, that it involves producing sounds mechanically and therefore constitutes a step toward the dehumanization of music. Machines after all are made and run by human beings and can—and frequently do—perfectly well serve human purposes. After all, too, the *organ* is a mechanical instrument, in the fullest sense of the word, and one which in its earliest forms, from all accounts that I have read, was extremely unwieldy and far less subject to human control than it became after some thousand years of development. Its development was brought about by men, for the purposes of men. Most of our other musical instruments, in fact, have mechanical aspects, however simple, which have been developed in the interest of greater range, greater plasticity, and even greater sensitivity—a more complete utilization, in other words, of available musical resources.

Finally, one last point regarding performance. It has perhaps, two facets, and let me state them as clearly as possible. A skeptical listener to all I have said might well ask, for instance: "If music is gesture, and if the gesture must always be a fresh one, and if there are thus, by implication, so many possibilities, how then can one possibly set up criteria that give one the right to call one performance good and another bad, or less good?" On the other hand, he might put what is essentially the same question in quite other terms, for instance: "Let us grant that music is ultimately gesture and movement, admittedly with all the human implications roughly outlined in the last chapter, necessitating constant renewal. But if this is true, what and where is the music itself, which, we are told, possesses real identity, which can be said to endure, and, in the case of some very great masters, *has* endured?" These are serious questions, after all, and very crucial ones—and the answers are not so easy as might be supposed. Ultimately they reduce themselves to the question: what does the performer really do, and how much is rightfully his, and how much rightfully the composer's?

Perhaps I might approach this question by recounting an experience I had some years ago, when listening to a concert in one of the European capitals. On the program was one of the two cantatas of Anton Webern—since the performance was in no way memorable, I have forgotten which. I did not have the score with me, and so it is possible that I am wrong if I say that it was letter perfect. Literally speaking, it probably was not, quite—simply by the law of averages. In any case, however, it was sung and played by professionals whose competence was obvious; the pitches were clear and secure, the ensemble excellent, the dynamics and tempi clearly defined; it obviously had been conscientiously prepared. But I might be tempted, and perhaps I was—I don't remember—to say "everything was there except the music." During the intermission I happened to meet a friend of mine from Princeton—an admirable and experienced musician whose collaboration I have enjoyed on several occasions in connection with performances of my own works. Discussing the performance of the cantata, we agreed that it was astonishingly bad; and then she remarked, "The performance we gave, with piano accompaniment, with the high school chorus in Princeton last winter was so much better." I myself had not heard the performance of which she spoke, but I knew that the man who trained the Princeton High School Chorus had on other occasions achieved some remarkable results with it. I also trusted this lady's judgment. But I took her remarks as, obviously I thought, an enthusiastic overstatement. The cantatas are, after all, extremely difficult, and in an idiom that is still unfamiliar enough to have prompted me to doubt whether high school students in their mid-teens could really cope with it successfully. Three months later, back in Princeton, however, I heard both cantatas sung by the high school students, and I then understood perfectly what she meant. One missed the orchestra, of course, and the performance lacked something, in intensity, in strong contrasts, and in boldness of outline, that adolescents, however well-trained, however talented, can scarcely ever be expected to give. They have seldom had the experiences that would make a fully satisfying achievement of these qualities possible. But they sang with fervor and dedication—and after all with remarkable accuracy, as they had been well trained to do. The result was that the music *was* there—one was really hearing the music of Webern. This is what I mean when I use the word "gesture." In the professional performance, it was precisely this—the music, its vitality and even its real contour—that was lacking. If one of the singers had, for instance, a wide interval to sing, one heard the notes, but was hardly aware of the interval itself—the connection and relationship between the notes. What was *lacking* was what I have called the *gesture,* and it was lacking pretty much throughout.

It is the *quality and character of the musical gesture* that constitutes the essence of the music, the essential goal of the performer's endeavors; but it is this, too, which in the last analysis—also, actually, the first—is most stubbornly impervious to what Stravinsky, in the passage I quoted previously, and in this identical context, called "verbal dialectic." It is that which the composer embodies in his tones, his rhythms, his phrases, his accents, and the larger episodes in which his music is designed. He does whatever he can to make his musical intentions clear; that is, to help the performer in grasping the outline, the inherent gesture, of the music. It should be clearly understood that this, and no more, is what musical notation consists in. The composer indicates as clearly as possible the nature, the scope, and the intensity of the gesture which he intends; but it remains for the performer to bring this gesture to actuality on each specific occasion. It follows that the performer's first task is properly that of *reading* the composers's music accurately. I use the word "read" here in its quite literal sense. Reading music, like reading words, implies not only hearing, in imagination, the sounds—or, respectively, the letters and the words—accurately, but also grasping the sense that the composer or the writer has used them to convey, on each relevant scale. The traditional musical notation does not, in some respects, entirely cover the needs and demands of today's music, though it remains a quite extraordinary achievement of our culture.

The basic problem of musical notation today is in large part a theoretical one, and belongs in the realm of musical theory rather than in that of notation as such. Very briefly stated, it involves the enormous changes that have taken place in music over the last three quarters of a century, and the fact that these changes are still taking place. Some twenty years ago— in 1949, I believe—I had a conversation with Arnold Schönberg in which we both agreed that it would be yet many years before the musical vocabulary of today could be adequately formulated in terms of musical theory; and it seems quite clear that, in spite of many brave attempts that have been made, the moment has not yet arrived at which this is possible in any but a piecemeal, or, at best, a very provisional manner. As far as notation proper is concerned, many attempts have been made by individual composers to find new ways of expressing their specific intentions. These are in varying degrees successful; but except in rather rare cases they involve specific types of music, and therefore are correspondingly limited in scope or application. Sometimes in fact they seem to be based on a not too clear understanding of what musical notation actually involves. The problems are formidable, first of all on the purely practical level. Musicians must learn to read music as fluently as we all learn to read words, and to react instantaneously and almost automatically to the indications with which they are familiar. If music is to be performed with the freedom and the flexibility which it demands, this must inevitably be so. If the performer, in other words, is to play the *music,* and not simply more or less mechanically to produce the notes, he must be able to free himself of the constraints involved in struggling unduly with the text as such.

As matters stand today, composers rarely if ever find themselves seriously hampered in making their intentions clear in terms of the existing notation. If we need new indications, we invent them and explain them fully. Part of our task as composers, obviously, is to master the notation: to know exactly what we mean by its various signs and terms and to use it accordingly; also, to make ourselves fully aware of the resources it makes available. Unfortunately, there is today a certain fairly prevalent carelessness in this regard, on the part of some composers and performers alike. But in any case, the composer's notation must be regarded—as a matter of course —as binding; and the performer must learn to interpret the inherent gesture in terms of it. This is the only valid meaning of the word "interpretation" in this context.

However, as I have repeatedly pointed out, it is the performer who brings the music to audible life, who, in other words, transmits the composer's musical vision, as the composer has conceived it in terms of gesture in sound. It is the performer who supplies the energy which is necessary to bring this about. Quite obviously he can do this only in terms of, or, perhaps better, through the medium of, his own personality. That is only to say that he must himself read the music, imagine it, and feel it before he can transmit it. If my words are really understood, it must be clear that by "personality" I mean something quite different from "personality" as it has sometimes been applied to performers. It does not imply and should not be allowed to condone any tinkering with the work on the part of the performer, for any reason whatever— not even for the conscious purpose of "endowing it with fresh energy." I have explained why fresh energy cannot really be supplied in this way. Variety as such is not the issue at all, and artificial attempts to achieve it often ruin performances. But since the performer is a human being, living and breathing, the fresh energy and the "personality" will inevitably be there. It is not something to be "put in" or otherwise applied from without, as a means of making the music supposedly more effective, more stylish in appearance, or, especially, more consistent with the performer's ideas of what his own image demands.

Styles of performances do change, of course, and I can recall, for instance, certain habits, almost universal in my childhood, which are virtually intolerable now. The habit, for instance, which even some of the greatest pianists cultivated, of putting the left hand down slightly before the right, intentionally and for expressive purposes, or certain cultivated habits of sliding from one note to another, on the part of string players. Such changes of fashion, I suppose, will always exist; and I can see no reason to take them for anything but what they are—prevailing habits of performers at certain periods. They do not, in my mind, impose any obligation on a performer to adopt such mannerisms in playing music written in that period. Too much stress is sometimes laid on historical exactness for its own sake. The important point is not how the music of Bach, for instance, sounded to Bach's contemporaries, but how it can be made vivid and clear to us or to others who will listen to it. This does not mean that knowledge of both the media for which any given piece of music was written and the habits of performance which were prevalent at the period may not be of interest and value to the performer of the piece in question. I myself find, for instance, that the keyboard music of Domenico Scarlatti suffers very much indeed when it is played on the piano rather than on the harpsichord; I rarely feel the same way in the case of Bach's music. Again, I feel that the changes which Wagner, Mahler, and others have sometimes made in Beethoven's orchestration were always unnecessary, always amounted to real distortion, and in some cases were disastrous. In Schumann's orchestral music, however, the actual writing presents real problems, which can be solved only by changes in the scoring, if the music is to be made clear. But I have heard performances by George Szell that, with very slight changes in dynamics, and with the elimination of certain doublings, transformed the otherwise thick and dull texture and revealed the genuine and fresh orchestral imagination of Schumann, which it has become traditional to deny or belittle. There are matters of judgment as well as of taste and fashion involved here, as in all such questions; and if the composer has furnished indications requiring a specific type of performance, the performer is as a matter of course obliged to follow them. Once more and finally, his overriding task is to present the music, its inherent gesture as transmitted to him by the composer, as faithfully and therefore as vividly as he can.

IV

Composing — I

It is worth recalling at this point that the distinction we make today between composers and performers is the result of a process of specialization that has been developing increasingly for approximately the last century and a half. In former times—until, roughly speaking, well after the time of Beethoven—composers were virtually always instrumental performers as well. The converse was also true, of course; and many individuals, including some of the greatest, achieved distinction in both capacities.

Until nearly the end of that period, the training of musicians was so designed as to include and relate both functions. As time went on the two activities—composing and performing—tended to become more specialized. The reasons for this are somewhat complex, and to linger over them would not only take me far outside the framework of this discussion, but would certainly also involve much detailed documentation that it is beyond my competence to furnish adequately. I believe, however, that even today both some training and some experience as a performer are vitally important for a composer. The reason I have mentioned this fact, of course, is that it is likewise vital to my discussion of composing, which is the subject of this chapter and the next. The first point to be made is the rather obvious one that the composer is, first and last, a *practical* musician. Obvious as this would seem, it is by no means, in this country at least, sufficiently understood in all of its implications. I remember quite well the time when people involved in musical education differentiated between "Music History and Appreciation," "Musical Theory," and *"Practical* Music." I used to wonder why the basic technical training of the composer was called "Musical Theory" while that of the painter or sculptor was called "Practical Art"—the word "practical" being reserved in the musical field strictly for performers. Such categorization was not invented in the United States, but as applied here it was not without its deleterious effects. Since the composer was very often naively regarded as a mysterious and romantic figure who worked under the guidance of a quasi-supernatural force called "inspiration," it occurred far too seldom to people to focus on the rather important fact that, like any artist in any other field, he must be a craftsman as well and that, no matter how great his gifts, his craft has to be learned and cultivated, not through "theory" in any real sense of the word, but through *practice*. The point may be illustrated quite simply through reference to any of the other arts. Clearly, for instance, no one can hope to become a poet or a novelist unless he not only knows the grammar of his language, but speaks and writes it with ease and with precision; these skills are barely the beginning, but are certainly the premise, of any achievement on his part. What we call "inspiration"—a word that has been considerably damaged through misuse, but still a viable one if properly understood—is of little meaning on any other basis. The point was made, rather bluntly if you like, but very effectively, in the reply of a distinguished French poet— Mallarmé, I believe—to a young man who asked his advice, saying that he was full of ideas, but could not find the words to express them adequately. The poet's reply was to the effect that poems are made after all not out of ideas, but out of words.

From a somewhat different aspect, I might illustrate my point with a very moving account I had, not so long ago, from a young and very gifted colleague and friend of mine, of a visit, a few hours before, to one of the large New York museums. He spoke of certain ivory carvings he had seen, and of his emotion and wonder in becoming aware of the intensity of the artist's love and involvement with not only the representation but the *materials* that these works manifested to him. I could think of no better illustration of the ultimate nature of craft, in any art. Indeed craft implies complete intimacy, to the point of identification, with the materials of one's art, intimacy to the point not only where the artist can shape them as he likes in service to his conception, but where he can do so without any difficulty arising from a lack of precision or fluency in the handling of them. I am, of course, not speaking of what is often called "facility," as the term is pejoratively applied, for instance, to composers who produce a great deal of music, with apparent ease, of superficial or mediocre quality. Many of the greatest works of art, musical and otherwise, have been produced very slowly, and many others very quickly, and the ultimate quality of a work quite obviously has nothing to do with either the rapidity or the slowness with which it has been created. A composer, or any other artist, may spend an enormous amount of time in finding the exact shape that he wants his work to take; the innumerable sketches that Beethoven and others have left, and the various versions that exist of works by many more composers, demonstrate this very clearly. But finding the exact shape is itself possible only on a basis of genuine fluency; otherwise the composer is merely thrashing aimlessly about. Beethoven himself *improvised* fluently, we are told, as the composer-performers of his time were trained and expected to do. Today also, the composer must possess the ability to put tones together easily, coherently, and with precision, in his head, if not at an instrument.

The point I am making is that a composer is first of all a person who has, as the Germans are wont to say, *Noten im Kopf*—"tones in his head"—constantly, either completely on the surface of his consciousness or barely below it. Composers are not, of course, unique in that respect; in fact, the first time I heard the German expression I have just quoted, it was said to me about a very distinguished performer, by his wife. There is nothing inherently mysterious about this faculty. Anyone who remembers any tune obviously sometimes has "tones in his head," and perhaps more often than he realizes— not only tones, but remembered snatches of melody and rhythm which he has to some degree made his own.

In the case of the composer, the process is constant and all-pervasive; it can be said that tones and rhythms—musical patterns which he improvises—are somewhere in his mind at virtually every moment, and that these can be brought at any time to the surface of his consciousness without any difficulty whatever. I am not implying that by any means all or even most of these patterns are significant or fruitful ones. Composers—even, presumably, the greatest ones—have their idle and desultory thoughts, as does everyone else, and in any case only a very small fraction of what goes on in a composer's mind actually finds its way into his compositions. At this point I am not speaking of composition as such at all, or even the beginning of it. Let me carry the point a little further. The composer is constantly improvising, as I have said, musical patterns. He is frequently, in fact, working them over, shaping them, and elaborating them. This last activity, as far as I can tell, is never a quite subconscious process, though in certain states of mind it can become an almost obsessive one. I am also fairly sure that the recollection of music that he already knows—even his own finished works—always is for the composer fully conscious from the start, or else it immediately becomes so by arresting his attention. This is true even when he cannot immediately "place" the reference. The reason for this, perhaps, is that, being already complete, the remembered fragment demands and in fact permits no formative activity on his part. One finds oneself no longer improvising, but *following* and recognizing. The whole psychological process is shifted; one is no longer making musical gestures of one's own, but rather enjoying and savoring those already completed, either by others or by oneself.

Let me stress here once more that I am talking about the manner in which a composer's mind is constantly ready for the activity of composition, and not yet about the activity itself. That activity can be said to begin at the point, which he can always recognize, when his ideas begin to crystallize decisively and to assume what is for him significant shape. This process may take so many different forms that it would be folly to pretend to give an adequate description of it. Furthermore, here as in every phase of composition, the composer is absorbed in the activity and not at all concerned with the process as such. For this reason he can only describe the latter in retrospect, and his observations, however eminent their source, are always to be taken as ex post facto. All I am saying is that a composer, like anyone else engaged in creative activity, is totally involved in *what he is doing;* only to a very peripheral extent, if at all, is he interested in *how he is doing it.* So, before I give a few examples from my own experience, allow me to caution you to regard them as instances of a process that is so varied and so elusive as to defy exact description.

Note first of all that I am speaking of the beginning of a composition. In my own experience, the initial musical idea has most often been the one with which the piece actually opens. In some cases this idea has remained unaltered from the start; in others it has undergone a process of revision, sometimes quite considerable, before reaching its final form. In these latter cases the impulse behind the revision has never been other than that of enhancing the character of the idea; and, in at least a few cases, this has taken place not at the beginning of the work of composition, but after the piece as a whole had begun to take shape. In a considerable though smaller number of my works, the original idea from which the work grew was not that of the opening of the piece, but something which I knew would occur in the course of its development. This has been always the case where I have written large works for soloists with accompaniment. In these cases I have invariably, though not on principle, begun with the solo part. There is no need to linger over any of these instances, which I have cited only to indicate how varied the process of composition can be, even in its initial stages. One point I believe can be made. To judge from my own experience, the composer's initial idea is most likely to come at a moment when it is quite unexpected. I would not consider this observation of much value, however, if it had not been confirmed by many other sources, musical and otherwise. The point to be made is that musical ideas never arise on soil that is not, in ways that I have tried to describe, prepared for them; nor do they seem to come except at times when one's mind is quite open, relaxed, and at the same time, I suppose, potentially alert. What I have sometimes called a "musical image"— a pattern of tones, which can mean anything from the simplest and shortest possible rhythmic or melodic or even harmonic fragment to something considerably more elaborate —will seize the attention of a composer, assuming for him a very clear and definite character and setting his musical imagination in motion along a very clear line that this character determines. It is the definiteness of the character and the "setting in motion," as I have described it, that constitutes the significance of the musical idea for him.

This initial idea may sometimes bring with it other patterns, sometimes of quite *contrasting* characters. I can recall at least three occasions on which this has happened to me. On one of these, two extremely contrasting ideas came to me in such rapid succession that there was never any question in my mind that I must bring them together as parts of the same design. I did so, in fact, considerably later, in the first movement of a large orchestral work, of which the form is conditioned directly by the contrast between those two ideas. On the two other occasions to which I have referred, I sketched at one sitting and in quick succession, the opening measures of all the movements (in one case three, in the other four) of a large work. In the first of these cases the sketches were made on the back of a concert program, during the performance of a work in which I lost interest. My attention strayed from the notes which were being played, without any voluntary effort on my part. Let me add that I had occasion, two years later, to hear both my own finished piece and the work that was being played while its movements were being sketched. Not unnaturally, I listened attentively, this time, to the latter piece, and was able to assure myself that no trace of it had found its way into my piece.

This last case, of course, illustrates very well the nature of a composer's absorption in his work. I do not mean to imply that the composer as such is exceptional in this respect—or, presumably, in any other except that of the medium which he is using. The composer, like anyone who is engaged in work that can be called "creative"—and I use that term in its broadest possible sense—does not do his work, or any part of it, simply while sitting alone at his desk, but carries it with him—in his ear, not his pocket—constantly. It is something to which his imagination may contribute at virtually any moment, whatever the occasion or the circumstances.

By token of the same faculty, the composer acquires, at least to a large extent, the ability to exclude completely from his consciousness the sounds that occur around him—even musical tones, provided these do not force themselves on him, as they may sometimes do through sheer insistence or, as conceivably might happen, through engaging his attention as something that he really would care to listen to. This ability is of course the result not of an act of will, but of complete absorption in one's own work, which is a necessary condition of creative activity. It is not that one "concentrates" on one's work; if this were necessary, the effort involved would seriously hamper the accomplishment. One is, rather, taken over completely and possessed by one's work; all else is temporarily excluded from one's awareness.

I have tried to give some indication of the way a musical work gets started in a composer's mind. My necessarily brief account has been far from complete. A musical idea, even the initial one that sets a given work in movement, may of course grow more slowly. The constant activity and cumulative experience of a composer also develop many faculties that could be cited to qualify, even considerably, some of the things I have said.

If I have made my points clear, however, such qualifications would certainly take the form of footnotes rather than objections. Some indications of their nature may be sensed if I pursue the matter a step further. In speaking of a musical idea and its significance for the composer I have stated that the idea seizes his attention, assuming for him a very clear character and setting his imagination in motion along a very clear line determined by this character. The composer's musical thoughts are, from this moment on *directed* by the line that his idea prescribes. In other words until the work initiated by this idea is either completed or abandoned, his succeeding ideas are most likely to have a very clear relationship to the main musical line of thought which he is pursuing. I have already referred, in Chapter II, to one instance of precisely this kind—where I knew exactly what I needed, in a certain work and a certain context within it, and was seeking the exact pattern that would embody it. In a similar manner, though generally with less effort, I have on many occasions had the ideas, even the prinicpal ones, for later movements of large works while I was intensively involved and actively at work in composing one of the earlier ones. Let me hold this point momentarily in abeyance, however, while I draw attention to the fact that one's musical thoughts may at times be in some degree directed in other ways than as a train of thought engendered by what I have called an initial idea. It may be directed, for instance, by a text that one wishes to set to music or a drama that one wishes to embody in music. Or, for instance, by a medium in which one has become interested. In my own work the most striking and, for me, bizarre of such instances had to do with a work that a friend had requested of me, but that I had, for what seemed to me the best of reasons, decided definitely not to write. The work was a sonata for unaccompanied violin—a medium which seemed to me at the time both unsuited to my musical style and technically forbidding. Some weeks later, however, I found myself mentally toying with half-formed fragments of violin music; and in due time, somewhat to my surprise and even consternation, musical ideas began to shape themselves, leading my imagination in a very definite direction; and it became clear to me that I must write the piece after all.

Given a clear and concretely envisaged artistic purpose, a composer can, it should be obvious, direct his musical thoughts in any way he sees fit. However, the principal idea that I have sought thus far to convey still holds; the real beginning of a musical composition occurs when the composer's imagination is set in motion by a musical pattern that has taken hold of it. It is even quite likely that most of what I have said so far could be applied, with a little change of vocabulary, to the workings of the mind in virtually any context, whether that be one which we customarily call "creative" or not.

I am tempted to stress this point for a number of reasons. The main one is simply the all too prevalent idea that the capacity for significant achievement in the arts is somehow sui generis, and that it involves modes of thought and action which are inaccessible and inconceivable to those of lesser talents, or engaged in other forms of activity. Years of observation, of reading, and of association with artists have failed to show me any evidence that this is true, and plenty of evidence that it is not. It is not the method or pattern of activity, but its content and its intensity, that ultimately determine the character and quality of the result.

In any case, I am convinced that the actual processes involved in producing music, or probably any other form of art, differ very little in kind from one individual to another or from one age to another. The personal habits—including habits of work—do differ, of course; but these are conditioned largely by outward circumstances, by personal idiosyncrasies, or by other essentially irrelevant factors, which vary even in the lifetime of any single individual without any demonstrable effect on the quality of his work. What is decisive—and overwhelmingly so—is the content of the artist's ideas and the intensity and single-mindedness of his involvement, and these are not in any way discernible in terms of anything but the result.

I am also convinced that the overriding qualitative factor in a musical pattern which turns out to be a genuine musical idea is little more or less than its significance to the composer himself. Here again I find myself obliged to return to the word "gesture." There has been much discussion, from time to time, regarding what constitutes a "good melody," or a "great tune," or a "good theme," and, correspondingly, the pejorative converse of each. I am not at all convinced that the answer to any of these questions can be found in terms of tones and rhythms alone, even though it should perhaps be easier to find definitions of bad musical ideas than of good ones. At the very least, the words "good" and "bad," used in this way, require a specific context if they are to have any real meaning; and the specific context can only be that which is already present, at least in a germinative stage, in the composer's mind. Otherwise we are simply confronted, in such a discussion, with another instance of the pitfalls of verbalization.

Another factor is relevant here, too: the critical faculty that the composer allegedly must possess. I would not at all deny that such a faculty exists. Certainly the composer can, must, and does make choices, and constantly. But I would insist that he makes these choices with reference to his specific intentions and the artistic realization of these; he does not make them on any basis that strikes him as in any way abstract. They are always choices, once more, made within a very specific context; and for the most part they are not of a nature as to require any deliberation whatever. The composer does not ask himself, apropos of what he is doing: "Is this good," "is it beautiful," or even "is it interesting"; if he should do so he would be quite off the track. What he is really asking is whether what he is doing is right, in terms of its specific context, which is that of his conception, to which his musical ideas have led him.

I find myself tempted here to draw the conclusion that seems logical at this point, and state that no possible pattern of tones in movement is inherently superior to another in terms of what a composer can make out of it if it strikes his imagination. Certainly many of our accepted ideas are faulty in this respect. Much nonsense, I feel, has been written about Beethoven's sketch-books; if considered attentively, it would seem to imply that Beethoven was awkward and incompetent even on a rather elementary scale, blindly groping his way from something hopelessly trivial to a very great result. As to the final result one must certainly agree; but I have often felt, in studying the sketches, that, had he felt so inclined,

Beethoven could have made a great deal out of any one of the earlier versions too. Obviously it would have been a different piece, and since that piece is not in existence, we can never know what it would have been like. I would recall also the very acute observation that Artur Schnabel was fond of making, that "genius begins to be apparent only at about the fifth measure"; and I must confess I can think offhand of many very great works whose opening measures, taken by themselves, I could easily imagine as having been written by virtually any competent contemporary of the composer's. Of course, genius has a way of exercising a retroactive influence as well as an immediate and prospective one, and as soon as we know where those measures are going to lead, they are transformed for us. After all, I am only saying that the material in itself is nothing without the imagination of the composer, which it sets in motion; and this much is certainly true. Furthermore, obviously Beethoven was never groping at all, but—and this is for me perhaps the most fascinating information that the sketches give us—working in a straight line toward that very specific and characteristic shape which the idea finally takes. He was not simply "improving" it by any abstract standard.

Let me return to the actual sequence of events in the process of composition. I have spoken of the genesis of musical ideas, of the musical trains of thought and imagination that they set in motion, and of some of the aspects that these may take. It is through these trains of thought and imagination that the composer's conception of his work takes shape. This amounts to what may be called a kind of preview of his work in its totality. He at this point has, in other words, become fully aware of the work's identity. He has established the main ideas and their relationship within the total design. As he elaborates the work further, he recognizes without difficulty and with complete precision what belongs there and what does not. This is true, I believe, at all levels, from the larger features down to the smallest detail. If I should attempt to elaborate further on what I have said, I would simply be listing the various elements that go into the making of a piece of music. Assuming, as I am doing, that the conception is adequately strong and firmly established, it will govern every move that the composer makes from this point on. His work has become essentially one of execution, and requires of him constant awareness of not only everything that has been done up to the point at which he has arrived, but of what is to come. Each move he makes will exert its influence on what is to follow, and as he approaches the end of the work it may well begin to seem to him that the work has become more and more, as it were, predetermined. His choices are made within a specific framework, which, as it grows, exerts an ever greater influence on what is to come.

In Chapter II, I made reference to a certain letter, frequently ascribed to Mozart, though its authenticity is genuinely in doubt. Whoever the writer, the letter does convey the clear impression of a man of extraordinary vivacity and, if every statement is taken literally, of gifts that seem virtually incredible. Both the tone and the content of the letter make clear that it is a generalized account of the process of composing, and of the way in which a composer's ideas develop, rather than a painstakingly accurate report of an essentially invariable procedure. What I am suggesting is that it is not the method of composing as such, but the *content of the ideas* and above all the result, that are of interest, even in the case of a composer like Mozart. Actually, my description of the process of composing and that in the letter are very similar, and for very obvious reasons; there is little else that can be said. One starts with an initial impulse, and it grows until the outlines of the conception are clear.

It is at the last-named point that Mozart's supposed letter has been sometimes considered problematical, though it is not for this reason that its authenticity is questioned. Mozart speaks of expanding his ideas more and more until he has the complete work finished in his head, however long it may be. He adds, "Then my mind seizes it as a glance of my eye a beautiful picture or a handsome youth. It does not come to me successively, with its various parts worked out in detail, as they will be later on, but it is in its entirety that my imagination lets me hear it." [1]

The precise meaning of this passage depends on an exact interpretation of the experience it describes. I must confess that I do not see any reason to interpret it in a manner that seems incredible. The first sentence I have quoted here suggests to me nothing by nature different from the kind of instantaneous synthetic impression that forms in the mind of anyone who recalls a person whom he knows, or a large and even complex object, or a work or art or a piece of music that he knows very well. It is, so to speak, an imaginative kernel that identifies the object with complete precision, and from which one, if and when one chooses, can proceed with ease to a contemplation of the whole, in accordance with one's memory of it. If we take the words in this sense—as it seems to

---

[1] As quoted in Jacques Hadamard, *The Psychology of Invention in the Mathematical Field* (Princeton, N.J.: Princeton University Press, 1945), pp. 16–17.

me entirely possible to do—Mozart is represented as saying only that his conception at that point is completely clear to him, and that what remains is, in his own words, to work out its various parts in detail. Obviously, Mozart was a man of unique genius; but his uniqueness was not of a nature that anyone—least of all, perhaps, he himself—could bring out in a description of his methods of work such as forms the subject of this letter. Whether or not he was its author, is it not perhaps a mistake to seek in every utterance of a man of genius, as has been done time and again, some kind of sibylline significance, and to forget or ignore the possibility that he was speaking, not as a unique individual, but simply, at a given moment, as a superb or even simply a highly competent craftsman? Once more it is the content, not the method, that is decisive.

I introduced this discussion, first of all, in order to illustrate more clearly what I have said about the whole process of composition. There are differences, of course, between the account ascribed to Mozart and my own. It seems to me, however, that the essential correspondence between them is still more striking. The reason for this is the very obvious one that it would be difficult to imagine any other way of composing. I am quite aware that some composers today lay claim to a more calculated approach than that which I have indicated; and I have no inclination to prejudge the result on that or any other basis. I would simply ask, on what basis do they make their initial and specific choices, both of material and character? I have even heard the statement, by a very young composer indeed, that every piece of music is a "theorem." That certainly is not very tempting to me as a prospective listener to his music; but I would certainly try to withhold judgment until I had heard the music itself. I would still ask the question, why precisely this piece and no other? And that is what is at issue here.

Second, I have introduced the putative Mozart letter precisely because it presents a vivid picture of what I have referred to as the "conception" of a work. The letter describes the process rather dramatically, in fact, and I have, since I am generalizing, carefully avoided such a tone. The essential is, of course, that one necessary phase of a composer's work arrives at a point, before the final execution of the work, where he sees it as a whole and knows where everything belongs. This process is very well illustrated in what, I believe, must be a rather frequent experience for every composer. One may look forward with a certain tension to some point in the work which one knows must come, but at which one has not yet arrived; and then one very frequently discovers, when one does come to it, that the problem has already solved itself. What this point illustrates, I think, is a fact that is inherent in the nature of musical thought, and indeed in the nature of music itself. I have already identified it as "controlled movement"—a term that implies movement toward specific goals. One can identify the essential fact of musical structure in these terms. Given his conception, the composer is constantly moving toward the various structural goals that, like the material texture of the music itself, are determined by that conception. The successive goals, in the same manner, form a larger pattern of their own, or, perhaps more accurately, successive layers of patterns, thus establishing the overall large-scale pattern. Lest this statement seem too abstract, let me try to illustrate it very roughly with two examples that are surely familiar to most people: let us say, the first movements of Beethoven's *Eroica* and *Pastoral* symphonies. I shall not go into any detail, since that is unnecessary for my purposes. It is quite sufficient to point out, in the most general terms, that while both are in recognizable "sonata form," they are in structural character and detail about as different as could be imagined. The *Eroica* contains many strongly contrasted themes, the *Pastoral* fewer and very lightly contrasted ones, which melt into one another so placidly that one is scarcely aware of them as distinct ideas, but perceives them almost as different phases of a continuous melodic and harmonic line. In the *Eroica* the various in-dividual features are frequently underlined by sharp rhythmic characterizations, of great variety, while in the *Pastoral* the rhythmic features pass from one to the other with the utmost smoothness. As far as larger features are concerned, the two symphonies differ sharply in all of the "standard" component features of the sonata form. In the *Eroica* they are all—exposition, development, recapitulation, and coda—elaborate, full of contrasts, and constantly in movement, while in the *Pastoral* they are always simple and at times almost static over relatively long stretches. And so on. What all of this signifies is that while both of these works can be characterized in terms of the same general overall scheme, they differ in every specific structural respect.

This leads me to another point, which I shall touch upon only briefly, reserving fuller treatment for the next chapter, in which I shall deal with certain questions that have more specific reference to our own time. The point is that, as far as the largest level of musical design is concerned, the possible basic patterns are fewer in number than is generally sup-posed. Let me make clear that I am not, in saying this, implying that we should continue to think in terms of "standard" forms. I have, I believe quite decisively, already expressed myself on this point. But if we think of large design in terms of its basic principles, rather than specific formulas, we will find, I think, that these principles are relatively few, as are the abstract formal patterns we can deduce from them. Their application, however, is infinitely varied, in terms of the materials in which they are embodied. We can speak for instance of *association,* through repetition or variation, of *contrast,* of *cumulative movement,* of *balance.* If we understand the first of these principles—association—properly, we can recognize it as one of the basic means through which musical unity is achieved. However, unless we understand it in its crudest sense, its application is in practice as varied as are musical materials themselves. In a given context the questions to be answered would be of the nature: "What degree of repetition is appropriate?" "What is the appropriate element through which association must be created, at this moment?" And a host of similar ones. Of course the composer does not ask himself these questions. First of all, as I have pointed out, he does not think indirectly in verbal terms, but directly in terms of tones, rhythms, and movement. Second, the context, and above all, his conception dictates the answer.

It may have been observed that throughout most of this chapter I have constantly made statements that imply something like a predetermined course throughout the whole process of composition. This reminds me of an occasion when I was berated over the telephone by a colleague because I had stated, in a program note to a work of mine that had just had its first performance, that I had sought always to be, as I think I put it, "the obedient servant of my musical ideas."

"What do you mean by that," he said; "You are not the servant, you are the master, of your ideas." I am afraid I think that his point is a strictly semantic one. Nietzsche once pointed out in a very beautiful passage in, I believe, *Beyond Good and Evil,* that the artist feels happiest and even freest when he is actually most bound—by his conception, that is to say, and by the limitations that he imposes upon himself in its service. This is a point, I believe, that cannot be too strongly emphasized. We hear a great deal about the freedom of the artist, and most of us agree that freedom is a good thing. Especially, let me add, if it is properly understood. Do we mean, speaking of the artist, that he should be free from governmental or ecclesiastical restraint? Naturally he should. Free from economic problems? Of course, insofar as this is possible. Should he be free to follow his own way, regardless of what are considered to be the "rules" or "conventions" of his art? Of course, this has been the traditional procedure of the greatest composers of every generation, even some of those who, like Bach were considered in some degree conservative in their own time. No fully grown man, it may be added, feels bound by rules or conventions as such, once he has outlived their usefulness for him; and, in the case of artists, every one who has mastered his art feels fully free, simply by virtue of his mastery of his materials, and in strict proportion to his mastery of them. He can do with them anything he chooses. I remember a book that appeared many years ago, entitled *Beethoven, the Man who Freed Music.* The question arose in my mind: "What did he free it from?" From Mozart, perhaps, or Haydn? I do not mean to labor the point; simply to draw attention to the fact that the artist— barring forces quite external to his art—*is* free, in proportion to his mastery of his materials, in every way that has any importance to him. He is free, that is, to make the music which is his own, that which he wants to make. Once he has clearly envisaged what this is, he must follow its demands. In so doing, he is enjoying the most intense musical experience that is open to him, and presumably he finds fulfillment in it.

V

Composing — II

IN THE LAST CHAPTER I touched upon the subject of musical design, and intimated that while its basic principles are few and the patterns, deducible from them in the abstract, simple, the possibilities in application are infinitely various. Let me try to illustrate this, in crude and, since I am dealing in generalities, abstract and hypothetical form. Let us imagine a composer setting out to write a piece of some length, although for our purposes the length need not be even very great. Let it be understood from the start that the composer I am imagining is quite fictitious. Not only has he no personal identity, but he is fictitious in a much more fundamental sense. I am ascribing to him an a priori verbal articulateness in regard to his immediate situation, which implies not only very much less real craft and less experience than a composer must have, but also a strictly critical and analytical approach to composition, which is the reverse of a creative one. A composer who is intent on writing music knows in advance the answers to the problems which I shall picture this one asking himself. Above all, such questions as a real composer does ask himself will be specific, that is, they will always present themselves to him in the form of musical images—actual patterns and relationships in sound and movement, heard or adumbrated in his imagination. I am therefore not to be understood as laying down rules or laws of composition but simply as attempting to describe in words some of the considerations which frequently operate in connection with the putting together of a large musical design.

Let us assume that our hypothetical composer, then, has begun a large work in a manner that satisfies him. He has come to the point in the piece where he feels that contrast is necessary. Note, please, that I have not made any specifications whatever, and, in fact it would make no sense should I try to do so. The opening phase I have suggested may be anything that the composer chooses, and may take any form the composer wishes. It may be essentially simple or very complex. It may be quite static or, on the other hand, very bold and wide-ranging in movement. It may consist in the intensive deployment of a single musical idea or may be composed of a number of varied ones. I am assuming only a basic unity of conception, intent, and direction. This may, and throughout musical literature *has,* assumed thousands of shapes, and will no doubt assume thousands more. What is of concern to our composer, at this point, is the nature of the first major contrast in the piece that he is constructing. The nature and the degree of contrast depend of course on his conception, and will to a large extent determine the character and the eventual form of the piece as a whole. The composer can choose his contrast as something entirely new or, on the other hand, he can decide to present the musical material of the preceding section or episode in a new guise. Let us assume that he chooses the former method. The moment will then certainly arrive when he feels the need of reaffirming the unity in the piece, by in some manner referring back to his opening statement or section. The most obvious method of doing this is, of course, that of more or less exact repetition; and this was, with some qualification, the usual procedure with the composers of what we call the "classic period." But even in the time of Haydn and Mozart and Beethoven this procedure was applied with considerable freedom. In a very general and therefore a very rough sense—very rough indeed, I have to emphasize—one can conclude that the smaller the dimensions, the greater the freedom. There is a completely logical reason for this. Since music is a temporal art, the smaller the dimensions, the less far-flung are the relationships involved, and, in consequence, the lesser the span of memory required in order to grasp them. This is, without any doubt whatever, the reason why some critics have regarded the sonatas and quartets of these composers as—and I have to use quotes—more "radical" or "free" than the larger symphonies and concertos.

At all events, the point at issue in this context is not that of exact repetition, but of clear and recognizable association. The composer is in effect asserting the unity of his piece through "back-reference" to an important element that has been already stated. This back-reference will obviously involve some element of repetition; but the degree and kind of repetition that is appropriate and necessary in any given case will depend not only on the scale of the work involved, but on its character as well.

It is for that reason, among others, that I prefer to use the word "association," and prefer to speak of "associative elements" rather than "themes." The term "theme," partly as the result of a still all too prevalent pedagogical inertia, has acquired certain rather precise connotations, which are even at variance with the original meaning of the word. Thus the word "theme," which normally denotes a *unifying structural element,* is often used to denote simply a melodic line that occupies the foreground at the moment. I have no interest in haggling over words; but I would point out that any musical feature—melodic, harmonic, rhythmic, textural, sonorous, or even merely dynamic—can assume the role of an associative element provided it have a clear identity and provided, of course, that the composer use it in a way that enhances rather than obscures the essential outline of the piece. If this statement seems somewhat vague, let me point out that the proviso which it embodies applies in fact to everything that I have said. Unless the composer knows exactly what he wants, unless he knows it, that is to say, in terms not of abstract formal schemes but of specific musical imagery—tones, rhythm, and the musical momentum that they engender— unless in these terms he knows what he wants and is able to bring it into being, no principles have any relevance to musical form in the actual and concrete sense of the word. This is only saying (with, perhaps, a fraternal nod to Mallarmé, whom I quoted in the previous chapter) that music is, after all, made of musical materials, not of preconceived ideas, even in the form of recipes or projects.

Let me return for a very brief moment to our fictitious composer, once more at the point where, having made an initial musical statement, he feels the need for a change. I spoke in that connection of "contrast." He has, at this point, a possible alternative method of procedure. Instead of introducing definitely contrasting ideas he may choose to present the same basic patterns, but in altered though recognizable form. He may, in other words, apply the principle of variation, which in our own time has come to play an extremely important and pervasive role in the techniques of composition. Obviously, in this case the principle of association assumes a somewhat different role, since there is no clearly definable question of unity involving a "return" to something that is continuously present. There are, of course, many levels and degrees of association, and a composer may and almost always does make use of these in the service of a specific long-range formal conception. But since such considerations are beyond the scope of my argument, I shall proceed to a few further comments and conclusions.

I hope it is clear that I am not suggesting that the well-known formulas "*ABA*" and "*A, A′, . . .*" solve all large-scale formal problems, or indeed any of them. I am only pointing out that, as far as the question of contrast, and unity in terms of contrast, is concerned, an infinite number of possible procedures can be subsumed under one or the other of these two headings. The letters *A* and *B*—*A* denoting *associative,* and *B contrasting* elements—can be applied, strictly ex post facto, to any conceivable situation in which these two factors—unity and contrast—are present. But the musician, and above all the composer, thinks in terms of the materials of music, that is to say, in terms of sound, rhythm, and of the patterns of movement that these elements embody. The letters *A* and *B,* as I have used them here, have no real meaning for him, but are simply verbal and descriptive symbols that may be applied, perhaps relevantly, to his work after it is done.

I shall return to this point presently, for I think it is a very crucial one, and for various reasons one which has to be emphasized in no uncertain terms in the United States and at this particuar moment. There are, however, two other points which must be made before leaving the subject of large musical design. First of all, the questions of association and contrast take on a very different aspect when the music consists in the setting of a text or of dramatic spectacle. Under the latter term I mean to include not only opera and ballet, but a number of forms allied to them, such as certain of our younger composers are developing today. In these works, obviously, it is not merely the musical elements as such that will determine the form of the work that results. The apparent caution of this statement simply reflects the fact, overwhelmingly evidenced in musical literature throughout the ages, that the relation between music and text, or even music and drama, can take, and has taken, a multitude—one is almost tempted to say, an infinitude—of successful forms.

The point is that text and drama provide associative elements that can in one degree or another supplement, mitigate, or otherwise affect the urgency of purely musical ones. These are provided not merely by the developing expressive content of the text, but by the quasi-musical elements —rhythm, intonation, and accent—in the words and phrases as such. In the case of drama or ballet, the above consideration is heightened and rendered more urgent by the multiple and very palpable demands of not only the inner drama but the visible theater as well. The problem, if one regards it as such, is finding the means of making use of the fullest possible potentialities of the various media involved, in the interest of a unity that will enhance the power and the essential clarity of each. Each element must be a fully relevant part of the whole, fully functioning in its own right but at the same time not fully complete without the others. This means that not all texts are equally suitable for musical setting and that the requirements of an operatic text are by no means identical with those appropriate to a spoken drama. It should also be clear that a convincing musical setting of a literary or dramatic text will inevitably be one in which the music has a convincing life of its own, not, certainly, independent of the text but, rather, fully coordinate with it. In both cases it is music that, in the immediacy of its impact, forms the more powerful vehicle of expression and characterization. No matter how high the quality of the text, a vocal work stands or falls on the basis of its music; and while many operas have remained alive on the strength of the music alone, it would be hard to find one that has continued to enjoy vitality on the strength of a superior drama set to inferior music. The associative elements of a purely musical nature therefore retain a large degree of importance in the musical setting of a text or drama, even though the character of the contrasts is determined, and certain important and large-scale elements of association—the continuity of the plot, the identity and development of the characters—are provided by the drama.

I have felt obliged to discuss the questions of contrast and association at some length because of a widespread tendency to dwell on these processes, to define so-called "standard forms" in terms of them, thereby giving them preponderant importance in defining the nature of musical form itself. There is certainly no question of the importance of the associative factor. But one misses the essential point if one tries to define it in any terms save those of association as such: that is, of a clear reminder of something characteristic that has gone before. One may very well emphasize the fact that musical form has no meaning whatever except in so far as it is evident in the actual experience of the listener—not the casual listener, of course, but the one who really knows the work. Musical form is something to be felt and perceived, and recognized, first of all as *sensation*.

As far as the composer is concerned, an obvious and essential part of his task is to see that the outlines of his conception—the pattern of gesture, of which it consists—are clear. Thus the questions of continuity and articulation are even more fundamental, perhaps, than those of association and of contrast. Continuity, in fact, is implicit in the very definition of music; after all, continuity might almost be considered synonymous with time itself. As we apply the word continuity to music—at any rate, as I am applying it here—it denotes not only the consistency and logic of movement and its component patterns, but their character as well. Under its heading would come the relation of each tone, sonority, or pattern, each color or nuance, to what precedes or follows it, the nature of the transition between one rhythmic unit and the next, and hence their specific relationship. Within its sphere belong all questions of proportion and balance, of tension and relaxation, of the necessity or the effectiveness of a given contrast at a given point. More than any other element, except perhaps individual patterns as such, continuity determines the ultimate character of music: whether its basic movement, in its various aspects, is tense or relaxed, square or asymmetrical, whether the musical gesture is large or small, long or short of breath, and whether the details contribute to the character of the larger line or are simply held together by it. It is the element which determines one's judgment in such matters as whether a given piece is either longer or shorter than it should be, in terms of its effective design; whether it really moves ahead and sustains its interest; and ultimately whether the whole is convincing as a single large gesture or whether on the other hand it falters and moves only by fits and starts. Obviously what I am describing is not derivable in any real sense from technical devices or principles as such. Those which the composer utilizes in the service of continuity will obviously contribute to its character and its definition, but cannot of themselves insure its achievement. The latter can only result from the composer's creative effort; for continuity in any given case is a specific and characteristic aspect of the music, not a generalized one. It is the composer's gesture on its largest scale—as much a part and a product of his musical vision as are the musical ideas from which it is developed.

Closely involved with the principle of continuity is that of articulation. I have sometimes described the nature of musical structure as consisting of various levels, groups of smaller units which are so designed that on another level they combine into larger units, and so on until the overall design is reached. Each of the groups exercises, of course, its appropriate function in this design. The description is crude, and perhaps suggests a more regular and formalistic picture than the musical reality often presents. But proportion and equilibrium in music are the result of so many different and subtle factors that no scale of measurement can accurately account for them.

The analogy with verbal discourse, with its divisions into words, phrases, clauses, sentences, paragraphs, topics, and chapters is an obvious one; and as we are aware, the words "phrase," and—less regularly—"sentence" and "period" are applied to music also, although loosely and without any real uniformity of definition. We speak as well of "motifs," "themes," "sections," and "groups"—even of "musical ideas" —to denote, with equal lack of uniformity, rhythmic units of varying sizes. I need not belabor either these words or their definitions; after all, I have devoted a whole chapter to the pitfalls of musical terminology. Let me keep to the term "gesture," which I have favored throughout this book, and point out once again that the smaller gestures of which music consists at the outset group themselves to form larger units of gesture, and that these larger units similarly combine into still larger ones, until the entire overall design is complete. It is on this basis that contrasts and associative elements are organized and that the continuity of a musical work is achieved. It is of the greatest importance, therefore, that each of these component elements be given the clearest possible definition, in terms of its function, and this is the principle to which I have referred as *articulation*.[1] Note the phrase "in terms of its function." Let me give a very familiar example of what I mean. As I pointed out earlier, Haydn and Mozart, in their works of larger design—symphonies, concertos, chamber music, and sonatas—were developing musical resources that were still quite new, and in fact it was these resources that made possible the new dimension of musical design embodied in these works. Since their conception of musical design was a new one, they obviously felt it necessary to give the basic outlines of their forms the sharpest possible definition. I am convinced it is for this reason, and not for any other, that the music of this period, and especially that of its greatest masters, was characterized not only by very clear-cut phrasing but, at moments of importance in the structure, by emphatic and, frequently, several times repeated cadences. Points of lesser structural prominence receive correspondingly less emphasis. The composers were motivated, in other words, not by considerations of style—not, at least, in the superficial sense of the word—or fashion, but by the necessity of driving their structural points home as clearly as possible. With Beethoven, who followed them, the points are of course established just as clearly, but—undoubtedly because the

[1] The word "articulation" is also habitually applied to certain aspects of performance in a sense that is quite different from that used here.

materials and the procedures that they engendered had become more familiar—these points are frequently made in a less outspoken manner. Phrases are more frequently and more subtly elided, often in the service of a larger design; cadences are established just as firmly but not cut off so sharply from the surrounding material; and transitions become in a sense more subtle. These matters, it should be unnecessary to point out, have nothing to do with the relative genius of the composers in question, but pertain simply to the necessities of the situation as it appeared to them in the context of the moment.

Translated into terms of our own time, the specific means which these composers and their later followers had at their disposal seem no longer appropriate—if only because they were so richly exploited by them and by several generations of composers who followed them. These means have long since reached the status of clichés, as far as their further exploitation is concerned. The need for clear articulation, however, is as clear as ever; it is the primary means through which music takes shape, or we may say, makes sense, and composers have found themselves obliged to discover other means, implicit in our own vocabulary, by which to achieve it.

Before further discussing the elements of musical structure, it seems to me relevant to go back once more to the theme that I have repeatedly stressed: namely, that composers think in terms of musical sounds, not of words or of verbal concepts. All that I have been saying amounts to an attempt to describe in verbal terms the considerations which move a composer in terms of tones—that is, some aspects of what can only be called *thinking* in musical terms. Continuity, articulation, even association as I have tried to demonstrate it are goals to be achieved only through a sense of what I would insist on calling musical logic. It is a logic that proceeds from the premises of a given situation, through a chain of successive consequences, to a desired result, and this must certainly be called thinking, even at times very clearly calculated thinking. Yet it is thinking in which words are at no time either relevant or effective. I heard recently, for instance, a performance of *Das Rheingold,* and among many moments that especially struck me (I had not heard this work for many years) was the simple but beautifully realized transition from the end of the first interlude to the beginning of the second scene. It involves the conversion of one leitmotif into another, of very different character and significance. A most striking and, if one knows the drama and the music, an extremely telling relationship between two different dramatic elements is thus set up and made very clear. It would be quite impossible to pretend that Wagner was not fully conscious of this. The transition is accomplished by an association of melodic patterns which are very similar in form but quite different in character. The processes of perception and thought that went into its accomplishment—being in this case very simple and even obvious—can be pointed out very easily in words, as I have done only sketchily. But it is impossible to think of them as taking place in any sphere except that of direct auditory awareness of the musical sounds and momentum themselves.

I have referred to this very simple example in the hope that it may help to make clear what I have to say regarding the whole creative process in music. The elements of which I have spoken—contrast, association, continuity, articulation, proportion—are not factors of which the composer at his work thinks in the abstract, but rather words that roughly symbolize and classify the immediate demands that his ear makes in concrete musical situations. They do not even present themselves to him, generally, as separate demands, except in the most limited and momentary sense. Each element becomes effective in terms of all of the others, and they are by this token facets, or aspects, of the essentially organic process of making music. One may represent them therefore as identifiable factors, of which the composer is seldom conscious as such, that impel his ear in the desired direction in terms of musical result.

The antithesis between the creative and the analytical attitude toward composition has become a vital issue today, since musical analysis has come to enjoy a vogue of a kind for which I at least know no parallels in the past. There is no question that a composer can learn, as we know that great composers of the past often have learned, a great deal from studying the works of other composers, both predecessors and contemporaries. This is especially true in the case of young composers, of course. What one is sometimes tempted to regard as quasi-pathological is that musical analysis as sometimes practiced today has, like many other things in our present-day world, often tended to become overspecialized, something to be pursued for its own sake, often with the implied object of discovering and establishing the ultimate criteria of music on a quasi-scientific, supposedly rational basis. Concessions, however, are made, somewhat grudgingly, to what is called "intuition" as a quasi-explanation of what cannot fully be explained in strictly analytical terms.

It must be pointed out that analysis cannot reveal anything whatever except the structural aspects of a completed work.

What is called "intuition"—quite inaccurately, if the word is used with regard to its original meaning—is simply a result of the intensive and pertinent functioning of the aural imagination. This has nothing to do with "rationality" in an analytical sense. Discoveries after the fact are necessarily verbalized in terms of preexistent contexts. In composition, the composer's ear creates the contexts; it *hears forward,* as it were, in terms of the contexts. What I have called logical musical thinking is the consequential working out of a sustained musical impulse, pursuing a result constantly implicit in it. It is not in any sense a shrewd calculation of what should, in any theoretical terms, happen next. The aural imagination is simply *the working of the composer's ear, fully reliable and sure of its direction as it must be, in the service of a clearly envisaged conception.* The conception, developed in consequence of the musical ideas with which the composer has originally started out, is the premise of everything that happens in the work which he is composing; the latter is in fact the conception's realization and its embodiment. The conception is itself a musical image, and in bringing it to fuller realization, the composer is not pursuing a line of reasoning, but producing an object—an object not in space and made of solid materials, but nonetheless an object, in time, and composed of what I have called gesture. In the process of creating it the composer will be thinking, in terms of musical materials; but his musical thought is governed by the object he has envisaged and that he wishes to bring into being. If he writes, let us say, a canon, it will not be for any reason other than the fact that a canon belongs in his design. In other words, he is pursuing a creative goal, not one which he can achieve by simply pursuing a line of rational thought.

It is the creative result—the musical gesture at whatever level the work in question demands—and not the processes by which it is reached, that matters.

The reader will perhaps have noted that I have not used the word "inspiration" except very briefly in order to record that it is still a viable though much abused word. I have avoided it purposely until this moment, because I believe that it *has* a genuine and relevant meaning. One thinks of it often as something that comes in occasional and intermittent flashes, and of course the flashes do occur—not only to composers and artists but to others as well, in other terms. I have described, as well as I can, how a composer receives his musical ideas, and this is certainly one of the forms taken by what is called inspiration. One should remember, however, that an artist needs inspiration in every move he makes in his process of creation, and feels himself abandoned when he does not find it there to help him. For in essence it is nothing more nor less than the fund of extra energy that he needs if he is not simply to fall back on routine—or, still more unhappily, artifice— but is to bring to his work at every moment the intensity of imagination that it demands. If what I have said is clearly understood, it should not be difficult to understand the real issues which underlie the popular clichés about the heart versus the brain. Every composer whose music seems difficult to grasp is, as long as the difficulties persist, suspected or accused of composing with his brain rather than his heart—as if the one could function without the other. Flippancy aside, however, it is really not very clear what precisely is meant by this. Composers, like other artists and certainly like every human being who is deeply involved, throw all of the re-sources they possess—intellectual as well as emotional—into their involvement; and genuine involvement, after all, is primarily a matter of the heart. Involvement with music simply means that one loves it, and the involvement of the composer means that one loves to make music, loves its materials, and, as one says nowadays, identifies with it, heart and brain and body and soul. This is what composing eventually implies, and in any case the real issue is the music itself, and not the putative psychological stance of the composer.

To resume my discussion of the elements of musical structure—I had been speaking of articulation, and had tried to illustrate my points by referring to Haydn and Mozart and then to Beethoven, and the care with which these composers insured that the various structural elements of their larger works were thrown into adequate relief. I pointed out that the means by which they achieved this were exploited so thoroughly, by themselves and by several generations who followed them, that these means gradually assumed the aspect of clichés, in terms of which fresh musical ideas could no longer take adequate shape. The story of how this came about has often been told, and there is no reason for me to sketch it here. But I recalled that the need for clear articulation is as imperative as ever and that composers have therefore found themselves obliged to discover means of achieving it in terms of today's musical vocabulary.

Clearly, such means *have* been discovered, by individual composers in their own respective manners; and not merely the discoveries themselves, but the necessity and process of discovery, have very strongly affected not merely our musical vocabulary, but our ideas of musical form. Articulation, in the contemporary idiom, has been achieved, for instance, to a large extent by means of the organization of small-dimensional contrasts, in greater profusion than was the case in former times. It has been achieved also by various rhythmic means, not in themselves perhaps new but new in the extent and manner of their usage. By means of relevant types of phrase-structure, sharply defined; in terms of the rise and fall of the melodic line; and by acute awareness of the element of pacing, by which in this context is meant such things as the distance, if any, in time between the end of one phrase or section and the beginning of the next: the timing, so to speak, of the various musical events.

There are, of course, harmonic factors involved also, and certain topics must be noted which relate to them and to the question of musical structure in all its various aspects. Of all of these the most fundamental and most important is certainly the problem of tonality. This is no longer the burning issue that it once was, and I would not be discussing it here at all were it not for the fact that the process through which its urgency has evaporated is a rather curious one, based on a considerable degree of verbal confusion. There was a time when "atonality" was a slogan of the avant-garde, as it was originally a word coined, by the opponents of new music, as a weapon against the latter. It is in any case a very poor word and has been frequently recognized as such; poor first of all because it is a negative term, and thus indicates only something that is absent, while giving no indication of what—if anything—is present. It is therefore far more effective as a term of abuse than as a slogan, unless possibly as a gesture of defiance.

It is there, however, and there is little that can be done about it except to try to use it in ways that give it as much sense as possible. Unfortunately that, too, is difficult, and illustrates, better than any other example I can think of, the problems involved in using words to deal with music.

Consider, then, the word "tonality." It is the term denoting, very adequately, the principles according to which, for some three hundred very important years, musical tones and their relationships were organized into significant and intelligible patterns. Its principles were clearly and simply formulated, and they were flexible enough to embrace without undue difficulty the musical vocabulary as it developed, say, from Monteverdi to Bach, from Bach to Beethoven, and from Beethoven to Wagner and Brahms and Verdi. As early as the middle nineteenth century, however, some signs of real strain began to appear in the work of some composers—certainly in the music of Wagner and Liszt there are passages, even of considerable extension, which, though certainly composed with the principles of tonality as a point of departure, are not satisfactorily explicable on the basis of tonality alone. Among the composers who followed the last-named, the strain became more visible, and some—Debussy, for example—began to regard the principles of tonality as a shackle to be thrown off. The interesting thing is that Debussy is regarded today as a "tonal" composer, or at the very least not as in any sense an "atonal" one.

The point I am making is that tonality has come, in the eyes (or should I say the ears) of very many, to be identified, quite subjectively after all, with music that one finds intelligible, in which one can sense all of the relationships; and atonality with music that one does not find intelligible. There are, of course, those who prefer music which they do not quite understand, and are suspicious of that which they do. I am speaking quite seriously. A young colleague and friend of mine, who is unimpeachably of the avant-garde and at the same time not only a first-class musician but also a highly intelligent and sophisticated human being, recently told me of a young composer who, after a performance of my friend's work, approached him and said, with evident disapproval, "Why, that sounds *tonal*." My friend told me, "Do you know what I said to him? I said, 'Oh, thank you.'" In similar vein, I read somewhere, not so long ago, a statement, apparently by an admirer of Arnold Schönberg, to the effect that the latter had in his music abolished relationships between tones.

Needless to say, Schönberg did not do this, nor did he intend to; and, of course, as the saying goes, it would take some doing. The relationships between tones are nothing more or less than the musical intervals, both in an immediate and a far-flung sense; and since we are familiar with them—there are not so many, after all—and aware of them through virtually all the music we have ever known, they become quite real for us every time we hear two tones in succession. To "abolish them" we would have either to abandon the use of tones altogether (even that would not be so simple as it might seem) or to sound one note at a time and, before sounding the next, wait patiently until all memory of the first one has securely vanished. Patterns of tones, then, become memorable because we are aware of not merely the tones, but the intervals and the relationships that successions of intervals establish. This is the premise on which the principle of tonality was based, and for the reasons I have just stated it remains a basic premise today, even though the principle of tonality has been superseded. This is not a statement of belief or policy, but of stubborn fact. By the same token it follows that the better we know a piece of music, the clearer it becomes to us, and, if we have continued, consciously or other-wise, to identify intelligibility with tonality, the more "tonal" it seems.

Clearly, then, the organization of musical sound must inevitably involve patterns in which intervallic relationships play an important role. It is this consideration that has led to the dodecaphonic or twelve-tone principle as developed originally by Schönberg and his followers, and later by composers in virtually every land. How little its nature is understood is, unfortunately, evidenced by abundant docu-mentation. I shall give only one example of this, on which I stumbled recently while perusing a very well-known diction-ary. My eye caught the word "dodecaphonic" and I read "composed through the mechanical application of a partic-ular numerical arrangement of the notes of the chromatic scale." I need hardly say that "dodecaphonic" means nothing of the sort. Dodecaphonic composition is not "mechanical application," nor is the arrangement of the notes "numerical" or even what is implied in the word "arrangement"—not, that is, in any manner that makes sense. I might even go further and say that nothing that is implied in such terms can be called "composition" in any real sense of the word. I am not, of course, implying that the notes in the tone row cannot be identified by numbers—the notes of the diatonic scale have been so identified for the last two and a half centuries, after all. Nor am I implying that the tone row itself, and the order of its tones, is of minor importance. I am merely stressing the point that the tone row is an organic pattern of sounds and intervals, created by the composer's imagination in terms of sound and of the relationships be-tween sounds; it is a framework of reference the composer establishes for specific purposes—just as the composer of a larger work decides in advance the instrumental or vocal combination for which he is writing. It is in other words the composer's ear, not arithmetic and not dogma or theory, necessarily of an arbitrary nature, that is involved here.

The existence and even the logical application of dodecaphonic principle do not, of course, guarantee that it will be applied creatively. The point is simply that it was designed in order to provide composers with a basis through which they could find answers in principle to certain compositional problems; and the fact that it has done so in a fairly considerable and distinguished number of cases is not only ample justification for its existence, but in reality the *only possible* justification for any such principle.

What the dodecaphonic principle involves is the adoption of a basic pattern or series, containing all the available tones, hence a pattern also of intervals and relationships, as a source or frame of reference from which are derived all of the main structural elements in a given piece of music. This pattern is what is known as the tone row, the series, or the basic set; and the composer—assuming, as I have done throughout this whole discussion, that he is really composing and not merely toying with notes—chooses it, once more in terms of actual sound, as a means to a concrete musical result that he intends to achieve through it. He chooses it, in other words, for a creative purpose, and there are no rules whatever governing its choice. I have talked with many composers regarding this, and their answers have been invariably the same as my own— it comes to them, and evolves, just as does any other musical idea, in terms of a concrete and specific conception. The composer carries it in his ear—not, please note, simply in his pocket—and lets it work there of itself. From it he derives variants, of which the inversion, the retrograde series, and the retrograde inversion are the most obvious, since they retain most closely the melodic and intervallic relations involved. But he can derive other variants if he wishes, and use them as he chooses. Again, as he chooses, he can derive from the series—assuming that he has mastered it—an endless array of resources in the respective realms of association, contrast, continuity, and articulation. And if he has mastered it he will find himself not only thinking with spontaneity in its terms, but finding in it resources that he has not hitherto possessed.

I have discussed the dodecaphonic principle at some length not only because I have used it myself, but also in order to illustrate some of the directions in which composers of recent years have moved to confront the problems that they encounter in connection with the musical vocabulary available to them today. I do not imply, of course, that using this principle is the only means by which they can find solutions. The overriding fact is that the problems exist, and are real and concrete—problems of association, contrast, continuity, and articulation, problems which they must solve adequately if they are to achieve their creative goals, that is, to write music that satisfies them.

Let me close this chapter with a brief sketch of a composer's development as I see it. He will of course presumably begin with a strong impulse to compose, to put together patterns of notes and to find satisfaction in doing so. He will then, or should, feel the need of developing his abilities and resources in some efficient manner. If he has good advice, he will master his harmony and counterpoint, in exactly the same spirit as a performer practices his scales and his arpeggios—this is almost an exact parallel—and if he is fortunate enough to realize what thorough training means to him he will demand it of his teacher, not wait for the teacher to urge it on him. He will presumably continue his training to the point where he feels able to do exactly what he wants without it.

The next step will be what might be called a quest for identity. This entails not an avoidance of "influences," but the discovery and cultivation of himself, and taking full possession of all he needs. He must discover—and the process is inevitably a gradual one—who he is, in musical terms, what music he wants to write, what forms it must take, and he must work to bring that into being. He must bring it into being, I must emphasize once more, in terms not of his ideas of himself but of the actual music which he finds must come out. The two do not always quite correspond—as a matter of fact, at at least one point in my own development, they did not. The music, however, must win out, and the composer's self-image must yield and embrace it.

In a sense—if his development is a really healthy one—this process will continue throughout his career. He will have found his own way, have achieved his identity, but will continue making new discoveries, of kinds which there is no necessity to enumerate. The story has no convincingly predictable ending, of course, and in any case this has been a brief and very summary account. But I believe I can say that in pursuing his own way, and creating the music that he really needs to bring into being, the composer will find his greatest satisfaction and the only real inner security—it is, however, very real and very solid—that an artist can have.

VI

Criteria

One often hears the statement today, regarding the arts, that criteria have ceased to exist. One hears this, or something like it, from a variety of contradictory sources, embracing numbers of both those who believe that the arts have, to all serious intent or purpose, ceased, or are rapidly ceasing, to exist, and those who feel that they are flourishing as never before, and are rapidly moving to an ever more brilliant future. Naturally neither of these groups is unanimous on the subject of criteria; but the view that criteria no longer exist is widespread and, in certain quarters, taken for granted.

Let me state at the outset that I disagree, completely and profoundly, with all three of the positions that I have outlined above. I believe that criteria are as real as they ever were, and as definite in their nature. It is, however, quite obvious to all of us that the cultural situation in today's world is much more complex and more problematical than it has ever been before. Western culture has undergone a series of severe shocks—historical, intellectual, social, and technological—some of which can be traced back at least as far as the early Renaissance. In our own century there has been a sharp proliferation of such shocks. If we read the news thoughtfully it is quite easy to foresee that others, of quite a variety of forms and from a variety of sources, may still be in the offing, and that if we are to survive, culturally or even biologically, we must learn to adjust ourselves to them considerably better than we have succeeded in doing thus far.

The uneasy attitudes and states of mind that these events and prospects have induced in human beings have been amply publicized. I would not even mention them if they did not have a direct bearing on the subject of criteria and did not in fact form an inevitable background for any serious discussion of these, whether in terms of the arts or otherwise, today. For, manifestly, the very possibility of criteria involves the existence or assumption of some stable point or points of reference; and in a time of general uneasiness it is inevitable that all of the generally accepted ones should be subjected to the closest scrutiny and the sharpest challenge. This does not mean, of course, that they will inevitably succumb, or that they will even necessarily be weakened. It does mean, I think, that in so far as they survive, their terms will be somewhat altered, and that quite possibly the new shapes which they assume will furnish us with new perspectives in regard to not only the present but the past as well.

The process that I have just described has, in fact, taken place repeatedly in the past. We may even say that each composer of importance has to some extent established new criteria, or at least new nuances in existing ones; and this is true to an even greater extent of certain pivotal moments or tendencies or generations, whether or not these can be identified with any one individual. Certainly the present musical situation derives, to a very large extent indeed, from the composers of at least two generations previous to my own: the generation which produced Debussy, Ravel, Mahler, and Richard Strauss and that which produced Schönberg and Stravinsky and Bartók (and Berg and Webern). It was in the years covered by the active careers of these composers that the final break with the tonal system occurred and that new concepts of meter and rhythm, new concepts also of musical texture and color and, in brief, of all of the structural elements of music began to assert themselves. Clearly, these developments were inherent in the development of music itself. The composers simply dealt, each in his own way, with the problems of music as these presented themselves to them at the time. The composers themselves were aware of this, and gave abundant testimony to its effect. As the years of their most decisive production recede into the past, it becomes more and more clear that they were right. What seemed, fifty years ago, a radical break with tradition appears now as much an inevitable phase of tradition as was, for instance, the period at the close of the sixteenth century, when developments of a similarly radical nature seemed to transform the whole aspect of music. The most common usage of the word "tradition" is a perversion of its truest meaning; for the musical tradition as represented by composers implies above all continuity in development, and hence constant *change*. In the cases of both of the historical moments of which I have spoken, the changes have seemed relatively sudden and drastic, and even arbitrary, to the contemporaries of the composers concerned. In retrospect one can see them as the result of tendencies which began to be manifest long before the situation had, as it were, ripened. To return to our century: when the situation *was* ripe, the changes embodied in their works by Schönberg and by Stravinsky and their immediate followers became inevitable if music were to continue to develop.

They coincided in time, however, with the beginning of the historical cataclysms of the twentieth century; and the technological, economic, and social changes that took place in the wake of these cataclysms have not only produced the malaise of which I have spoken, but have also altered the very structure of our cultural society in such a way that values have become confused. In regard to the arts, issues have been raised which, so far as I know, have never been raised before. Thus, as far as music is concerned, a critical or pivotal moment within the development of music itself has coincided with a period of immense cultural turmoil. To the perennial difficulties of understanding an essentially new development in music have been added a number of factors that, in a variety of ways, have served to confuse the issues. Certainly, we must include among the musical issues not only matters of vocabulary—by which term I mean to denote the acoustical and rhythmical materials of music—but also matters of syntax—under which I include the constructive elements. These matters are themselves products of the musical imagination, and thus derive from causes that lie deeply embedded in human sensibility, awareness, and experience. Like every other product of imagination, music is ultimately rooted in human attitudes, and interacts with these. The confusion lies not in the recognition of the facts I have just stated, but in a tendency, not entirely new to our time, but very much exacerbated during the last decades, to seek musical criteria outside the realm of music itself. The error lies first of all in the propensity, again not in itself peculiar to our time, for approaching the whole question of criteria from the wrong end—that is, by applying to it, from the outside, as it were, predetermined standards, whether derived from a fixed conception of tradition, or of historical necessity (music history, of course), or of theoretical or aesthetic dogma. Second, the error lies in the practice, all too characteristic of our time, of applying to music criteria which have no connection, other than at best a purely speculative or fortuitous one, with music as such. Under this heading I would put matters ranging all the way from political, social, and even economic dogma to the infusion of musical theory, analysis, and finally critical judgment with elements drawn from physical science, mathematics, or even certain far-flung regions of philosophy.

I have chosen my words with considerable care, and have no intention of withdrawing or modifying them. Let me, however, make my thesis very clear. I am not suggesting in any way that music is independent of, or unrelated to, culture in general. This relationship is indeed so profound that attempts to define or pinpoint it—from Spengler down, so to speak—seem to me generally quite superficial and imprecise. I also am quite aware that sound is, after all, a physical phenomenon, that mathematics is a supreme achievement of human imagination and ingenuity, and that philosophy aims, in the last analysis, at covering the whole field of human consciousness and bringing order and integrity into its operations. I therefore am not suggesting that composers—or their public—should avoid interest in, or contact with, anything toward which their interest or curiosity impels them; and indeed I could with only the slightest reservation go cheerfully along with the thesis that, in general, the wider a musician's awareness of all human concerns, the richer his imagination is likely to be. But the reservation, however slight, is still a crucial one, and one that lies at the basis of my whole discussion of musical criteria. For although all of the genuine composer's vital experiences undoubtedly find their way to his musical imagination, and are transmuted and synthesized there in terms of musical materials, it is in the realm of musical imagination, and there alone, that musical criteria are to be found. It is completely idle to seek for them anywhere else. What I have asserted, therefore, is not simply a new affirmation of the older doctrine of *l'art pour l'art,* which, if I understand it correctly, became a slogan of artistic isolationism in the context of its time, and which fulfilled its purpose as a reaction against Romanticism in its more highly colored aspects, and which had perhaps a certain nationalistic coloration as well (I have never heard the phrase *Die Kunst für die Kunst*). I am not talking or even hinting of the ultimate human functions of music, which I believe to be various and essentially beyond the scope of this discussion. What I have found a symptom of confusion is simply a prevalent tendency to seek musical criteria outside the realm of music itself. This, together with some of its implications, and the pitfalls implicit in any attempt to define criteria in any but the most general sense, is my subject.

It is worthwhile, I think, to begin by considering the manner in which criteria are determined. I recall a discussion of some twenty years ago, in which the opinion was seriously advanced that what the speaker called "Shakespeare's reputation" was largely the result of a conspiracy of professors of English throughout the academic world on both sides of the Atlantic. I need hardly say that this struck me as a fantastic and even rather picturesque notion, especially since the man who voiced it was himself a professor, though not of English but of social and political philosophy. I quote it because it is typical of a widespread assumption that artistic criteria are somehow established by fiat, and handed down by authority, academic or otherwise. This too, of course, is a source of confusion. No such authority exists, even though it is true that there are many people, both in the academic world and elsewhere, who claim it and even scramble for it. It would in many ways be a healthy thing for the state of music and the other arts if this fact were more generally recognized. The genesis of criteria is a vastly more complex process, in which the opinions, reactions, and tastes of no one individual, myself included, have much importance. If all of us would relax and face that fact, we could probably contribute more effectively to the development of real criteria. We could also then feel quite secure in our tastes, and be less stubborn in maintaining them after their relevance has passed.

Musical criteria, in the first place, obviously derive from music, and are perpetuated by music, and undergo constant modification and refinement as new music appears on the scene. Obviously, too, the criteria which prevail are established by the music which prevails. I suppose few people would dispute this, and thus far it is a simple matter. It is the mechanics of the process that is far from simple.

The crux of the matter is: which music eventually prevails, how does it prevail, and who is it that determines whether it shall prevail or not? Let me draw attention to the fact that the question is one of *music* and not of composers. I emphasize this point not because I consider composers unimportant, or choose to forget that it is they who write the music. But during the sixty years of my life as a composer I have seen, in the United States, what has seemed to me an overemphasis on the composer—both individually and collectively—and his problems, even, one might say, at the expense of attention to his music itself. Like many others, I have at times benefited from this solicitude. But it must be constantly emphasized that it is the music which composers write, and not the composers—individually or collectively—which should take the first place in our consciousness; and this is in many ways made difficult, even sometimes by composers themselves. Quite a number of factors in our cultural and social life and certain habits which they engender tend to give personalities and personal images precedence, both in the minds of the public at large and in cultural circles, over the works that they represent.

Let me give one example of what I mean. I remember at least two decades during which, with the exception of premieres, the larger public had the opportunity to hear virtually no music of Stravinsky or Schönberg except *L'Oiseau de Feu* (*The Firebird*) and *Verklärte Nacht* (*Transfigured Night*) —pieces which I do not mean to belittle, but which in no way represent the mature work of either composer. Yet at the same time, the preeminence and the impact of these composers, in terms not of these works but of their later ones, was generally acknowledged. This state of affairs is so typical that our musical life seems at times to take on an aspect of eerie unreality. My point, once more, is that musical criteria are derived from the *music* which prevails. To repeat the questions which I originally posed: What music prevails, how does it prevail, and who is it that determines whether it shall prevail or not? The last question is the most difficult to answer, and let me consider it first. There are various stock answers—some say "the performers," others "the critics and the music historians," and still others "the public," or simply "the people." Very seldom does anyone mention the composers, and, in the context of the present discussion, I would heartily agree. We composers, of course, write the music, and why should one expect more of us? To be sure, some of us have, as Artur Schnabel once said of Wagner, been inclined toward a military career, and have set out to mold the whole of music in their own image. They have never succeeded, if only because no one is interested for long in mere epigones, and that is what this kind of empire-building aims at producing. One might also add that the cultured world in general tires rather quickly of monopolies of this kind, and almost always tends to seek new sources of satisfaction whenever and wherever they are available. It tends, within the prevailing framework, toward inclusiveness rather than exclusiveness, and hence toward the expansion of the framework itself. However, one cannot speak of "the performers," "the critics," or even "the public" or "the people" in this connection either. Not only are such categorizations sloppy and inaccurate when used in such a manner, but above all what actually occurs has clearly nothing to do with the influence of groups which are clearly identifiable on any basis whatever. The growth of a composer's or of a style's recognition—and of the criteria which result—is the product of the attraction which the music exerts on those who listen to it attentively, who come to know it intimately and thereby become involved in it, to the extent of engaging themselves on its behalf. By this I do not mean anything necessarily very dramatic. One can perfectly well say "the music, little by little, imposes itself"—but it does so first of all through the agency of those who possess what I earlier called "willing ears." We all know that there are many people, among performers, among critics and historians, and among the general public, whose ears are not willing at all; but there are also among all these groups many whose ears *are* willing, and it is these who—simply because adventurousness and curiosity and imaginativeness are products of human energy and not of inertia—have the ultimately decisive voice. Obviously I am picturing the situation in oversimplified terms. I am not talking of an "establishment," or an "elite," or a group among which votes or polls could be taken, nor am I talking of fixed and immutable judgments. It is quite true that judgments, after considerable time has elapsed, do tend to become stabilized, and, if you like, even to take on the odor of sanctity; and this is the source of my friend's misconceptions about Shakespeare. But this is only because they are constantly ratified by common consent, not only by academic dignitaries (who as a matter of fact are just as likely to question them) but also by at least large portions of the public. What I am talking about is a logical course of events that I have seen operating—sometimes with rather startling results—over the past sixty years, and of which the operations in the past are amply documented. The key to the process is the "willing ear" of large bodies of music lovers, and anyone who possesses such an organ and such a faculty contributes to it.

A "willing ear," let me emphasize, does *not* imply an undiscriminating ear, but the contrary. Perhaps I should put this statement in a positive rather than a negative form: *only* a willing ear is a genuinely discriminating one. For, obviously, it is only a willing ear—as I have defined the term— that retains the energy to pursue matters to the point where distinctions become valid.

To recapitulate: criteria are to be found in music and the musical imagination itself—that is, in the tones and rhythms and the patterns which they form—and not applied from without, from spheres which have nothing to do with this; musical criteria are essentially derived from the collective judgments of all of those who genuinely love music, with what I might call a healthy, earthy love. I do not at all mean to imply that such judgments are unanimous, as they obviously are not; or that they pursue a straight and unaltered course. Quite the contrary in fact; they are subject to constant revision, and even the greatest masters of the past have their ups and downs in the general flow of musical history.

It is against this background that I comment on certain types of criteria which are now in vogue. But I must preface these remarks with a word of caution. The willing ear is, after all, interested in the music that composers create, and not in what they say about it. This fact is worth mentioning because composers are, especially today, very often asked to speak about music, even sometimes on occasions when they would be very glad to remain silent. Very frequently—perhaps even most frequently—they speak about the matters which are on their minds at the moment, and forget, or do not bother, to speak of those which they take for granted. These they have accepted, while hardly taking the trouble to formulate them, or even to be consciously aware of them. As I tried to point out in Chapter II, it is very difficult, in any case, to speak about music; and for a composer it can at times be especially difficult because of his intense absorption in what he himself is doing and his obligation to it. I point all this out not in order to discredit or malign myself and my colleagues, but simply to emphasize once more my main thesis. The criteria which apply to our music are to be found in the music itself, and not in anything we composers may say about it.

It should be still more evident that the "willing ear" is not in the least interested in music history, even though its possessor, in other contexts, may quite conceivably be so. This is only to say that, if we listen to music for the satisfaction it can give us—and I can think of no other reason why we should listen to it—it is only the music itself, not our notions of its place in history, past or future, that can give us that satisfaction. Another way of stating the same thing is, of course, to say that musical values and historical values are by no means identical, in spite of the fact that they ultimately tend to coincide, and do so to a very large extent. They coincide because it is the judgments made by the willing ears of the world that eventually determine whether a given work or composer is to get into history or not, and if so, whether that work or composer will find its place in the main pages or in the footnotes, and whether it is there because of the value of the music itself or because of attendant or even fortuitous circumstances. This point is worth mentioning because of the prevalence of many assumptions and snap judgments, mostly regarding contemporary music, that are based on a confusion of the two categories. It should be obvious to anyone that it is music which determines musical history, and not history, or any historical concept, which determines musical values.

I have in mind, of course, not only criteria based on conceptions drawn from the musical past, but those based on speculation regarding the future—or non-future—of music in terms of trends categorizable at any given moment. Such speculation can be interesting, perhaps, and certainly is not in itself harmful. But the future is, after all, by definition non-existent. It is a fiction which—since it *is* a fiction—is quite illusory as far as furnishing viable criteria is concerned. Strictly speaking, as we see it, it is not the real future at all; in reality it is a part of the present, in terms of efforts, of hopes, or of fears. The one thing about which we can be virtually certain is that when the future actually comes to pass, it will be quite unlike anything we expect. We can, of course, be aware of causes, and in many cases foresee the directions in which they are leading, if that particular trend should continue; but the result in terms of the general human condition, for a number of clear reasons, is unforeseeable. To take a very obvious instance: men have just succeeded for the first time in landing on the moon's surface; but what the long-range human effects of that achievement will be we cannot predict; we can only speculate, sometimes certainly to advantage, on the possibilities. We can also assume, for instance, that scientists will continue to discover more and more sophisticated means of synthesizing life in the laboratory. I look with considerably less than relish on the possibility that one day the younger generation might be produced by such means, instead of by what at that time will be called, I suppose, the "conventional method." I even take some satisfaction in the thought that, should that ever occur, I will presumably no longer be around to witness it. I take still more satisfaction, of course, in the fact that all of this is pure fantasy, based on possibilities that may well never be fulfilled. We are all of us aware of other possibilities, both long and short in range, some of them bringing cataclysmic results, others producing reasonably desirable ones. But in each case our visions of the future are simply, and very essentially, a part of the dynamics of the present; about the future itself we know, and can know, nothing.

To return to music: nothing can be sillier than the judgment "this is right, because this is the way music *is* going or *must* go." The paradox of the matter is that it is not merely normal but essential for the composer to tell himself, in effect, "this is right, since this is the music which I want to bring into being." For the composer, the issue is the choice between the genuinely "creative" and productive and the merely "modern" and essentially conformist. It is a question of deep-seated moral attitudes on his part, and may well represent the most decisive as well as the most difficult choice that he has to make. However he chooses, in the end it is the result and only the result that is pertinent. The point is simply to what extent the composer has created a vivid, bold, and somehow memorable musical image—a specific image, that is, in sound and rhythm and musical movement. If he has succeeded in doing this, the means by which he has accomplished it are of no importance and are no one's concern but his own.

Another superficially apparent paradox in this connection is that while music does not exist for the purpose of filling the pages of music history books, it is quite certain that if such a goal were the sole or even the principal concern of a composer, his music would be most unlikely to remain in those books very long, if it ever got into them in the first place. In any case, musical criteria are to be found in music, not in a category or context that lies outside it.

We often hear the query, for instance, whether this or that category of music is "still alive," or "dead," or "dying"—*the* opera, for instance, *the* symphony, *the* concerto, or chamber music. The relevant and realistic question would be whether and to what extent such categories were, in a musical sense, ever really "alive," or in fact more than just convenient folders in a mental filing cabinet. I recall a recent conversation with a very distinguished European composer who told me that his publisher had refused to publish any more symphonies. His comment was, "So I just call them something else." I have heard such questions asked constantly during the course of my own lifetime, and no doubt they were asked earlier, as they will be in the future. Obviously there is always some substance behind them, since older patterns are always being superseded by newer ones; and certainly the institutions that to a large extent have become identified with them have on occasion been compelled to transform themselves or disappear. But in terms of music, categories of the kind that I have mentioned have always been so flexible that any precise definition of their limits is necessarily an arbitrary one. It follows that criteria supposedly derived from them are also arbitrary, as in any case they are secondary to the main issue, which is the music itself. In regard to the future, we certainly can assume one thing—based solidly not only on the experience of the past, but also on the sheer logic of human events. Whatever is significant in the music of any one generation will surely leave its trace in that of the one which follows. The question at any given time, if one could possibly ask it seriously, would be not whether a given movement or tendency will survive or die out, but in what eventual form it will influence the music that follows it. This is what survival means. Obviously, life itself is change as well as continuity, and change is the one thing that we can justifiably foresee.

What applies with regard to music history applies of course to various quasi-scientific or analytical sources of criteria as well. The search for such criteria is not new to our time; since many generations back, for instance, there have been attempts to explain musical phenomena and hence to obtain valid musical criteria in terms of physical sound. The facts of acoustical physics have often been very helpful in providing insight into the nature of the materials of which music is made. But since music is a creation of the imagination, physics has no relevance whatever as a determinant of musical criteria. To say that the overtone series, for instance, must be, since it is presumably a natural phenomenon, at the basis and in the forefront of our musical vocabulary is very much like saying that tables and chairs and houses must not be built of wood, since Nature did not design trees for that purpose.

In our own time there has been a tendency to make a fetish of objectivity; and whether this is the result of the general insecurity or a symptom of the evident homage that we pay to what is generally regarded as the scientific point of view, it misses the point as far as the arts are concerned. It should, it seems to me, be quite evident that while so-called objective and analytical methods of thought can, if properly applied, sometimes throw light on what a composer has written and therefore, by inference, on what he has intended, they cannot be of any use whatever in determining its value. I am of course quite aware that there are those who would deny the relevance or validity of any so-called "value judgments" whatever, even in the arts; and this is indeed the ultimate logic of any thoroughgoing objectivist position. Yet it must be quite clear that value judgments are at the center of the whole experience of the arts, and indeed of imaginative activity of any kind. For imaginative activity is by nature selective; it involves decisions, courses of action, and choices. In music and, I assume, in the other arts as well, the choices are constant, and each one of them is a specific value judgment made not, certainly, in terms of value in the abstract, but in terms of the composer's creative vision. To label this process "objective" is, it would certainly seem, to torture words to the point of grotesque deformity.

What is true of the composer is true, certainly, of the willing ear also. Any kind of satisfaction that we get from the arts is as much a product of choice as are the creative processes of the artists who produce them. We make our choices, first of all, on the basis of individual inclination; we are drawn to this or that individual work, first, in consequence of what is available to us, second, on the basis of the impact that we receive from it. As experience accumulates, curiosity develops also, and sooner or later we begin to generalize. We also begin to communicate with others and to enrich our experience by comparing it with theirs, gaining fresh insight as a result of the process. Most of all, we become more and more familiar with what we know and have loved already, and if we have developed curiosity, which is certainly an integral part of any involvement with the arts, we apply our accumulated capacities for knowledge and experience to whatever fresh material is offered us.

The objectivist may ask, how then can one speak of criteria? The question is not only entirely legitimate, but is what we are accustomed to call a "good question"—and the answer to it, in precisely this context, is far more profoundly important than perhaps we generally realize. It involves not only the arts but, quite legitimately, all the deepest and most urgent human concerns. Once more, and this time not in a specifically musical sense, let me refer to the pitfalls of verbalization. If "objectivity" implies excluding, under the appropriate circumstances, our own personal predilections or prejudices, it is obviously an obligation, and a serious one. It involves first of all a high degree of self-knowledge and candor with ourselves, which is vitally important to us in any case, and which we generally achieve only through effort, both intellectual and moral, and through experience. If we do not know ourselves, we do not know what our prejudices are or even what we want. If, on the other hand, "objectivity" implies the necessity for complete and unassailable quasi-scientific security, it is something quite different, and we may well be attracted to it because it absolves us from this effort.

I have been told repeatedly, and sometimes by scientists of the highest authority, that such security does not exist even in science itself. But even that is beside the point. The essential is, once more, that the criteria by which we judge music are to be found in music, and the attributes which we expect from it; these in turn are derived ultimately from the needs or impulses that draw us to music in the first place. We can well afford to face the fact that there are specialized uses to which music is put today; if we live life under current conditions, we can hardly escape that fact. We hear music pretty much everywhere—blaring from apartment house windows, in churches, at parades and public ceremonials, on the radio and television in our homes, in shops and dentists' offices; in taxicabs, restaurants, night clubs, and elevators; in airports, bus terminals, and on airplanes, both before and after they take off, and so on. Each of the various uses to which music is put has its own criteria, most of which have little to do with those which are inherent in music itself; in some cases, in fact, they imply virtually an absence of musical criteria, or at least a drastic limitation of them.

What then is the nature of valid musical criteria, as opposed to criteria arising from the uses to which music is put, and on what does the validity of these criteria rest? I have stated that they are derived from music itself, and determined by the "willing ears" of people who love music—millions of these, scattered all over the globe. The reality and the validity of criteria depend ultimately, therefore, on the basic attitudes which these millions of music lovers—and above all those among them whose involvement with music is most intense, most experienced, and most disinterested—have in common. It is on the level of disinterestedness that one finds their largest area of agreement. I have found this to be strikingly true on numerous occasions when I have participated with groups of musicians from widely different national and even geographical backgrounds in discussions of various sorts involving musical judgments on specific composers and works. What has impressed me always has been the contrast between, on the one hand, wide areas of disagreement often revealed as long as the discussion dealt with generalities and did not refer specifically to music read or heard in common, and, on the other hand, the basic agreement that spontaneously developed when the same individuals were confronted with actual music, preferably read in common and at leisure, though also sometimes listened to and discussed on the spot. The result seldom was unanimity, but it virtually always revealed a conspicuous agreement on concrete and specific points. The agreement developed, of course, because the participants, confronted with musical facts, were able to recognize them for what they were, and were challenged by circumstances to ignore, at least for the moment, their involvements of a more personal or parochial nature. The agreement was, in the cases which I have in mind, the product of a disinterestedness that was the more striking for the fact that the individuals involved were artists whose primary obligations, like those of all artists, were to their own work and their own ideas. If by "objectivity" were meant this kind of disinterestedness, it could indeed be considered a valid source of criteria, as in fact it is. But those who today demand, and claim, "objectivity" are, consciously or not, attempting to impose criteria which have nothing whatever to do with the actual experience of music, and which are not to be disputed in terms of that experience. Their thrust is in effect a totalitarian one, directed in the final analysis against the musical imagination itself.

There are, of course, much graver issues involved in this point than is immediately apparent. What I have defined as the real source of criteria clearly depends on inclinations that men possess in common. I believe—it seems to me hardly disputable—that men still possess these inclinations in common; they are built into the structure of the human organism, and into the reflex actions that serve our vital instincts. Obviously, the human race is on many, very likely most, other levels beset by divisiveness of all kinds, bred by conditions inherent in the nature of our society, and nurtured in turn by many influences which find profit in divisiveness as such. This divisiveness is clearly the result of the impact of advanced technological civilization, the speed with which it has developed, and perhaps above all the formidable power that it has released, on men and women everywhere. Not only has this created—and also uncovered—vast and bewilderingly urgent problems; it has also brought in its train a multifarious and all-pervasive scramble for power on the part of individuals, groups, and communities of all magnitudes. Quite evidently, the drive for power tends often to take precedence over the human needs with which the real problems are ultimately concerned. A clear by-product of this state of affairs is the widespread practice, with which we are daily confronted, of attempting to manipulate human beings in the mass—on pretexts varying from the noblest to the crassest —as standardized objects. This process involves ignoring, by-passing, or systematically belittling not only human diversities but whatever traits or inclinations offer resistance to the promotional, technological, organizational, or even professional goals that are immediately in question, the latter being taken for granted as automatically productive of human well-being.

It is not difficult to see that the same tendencies operate in the sphere of the arts, and not merely in so-called "traditionalist" circles. For these reasons it is the more necessary to recall constantly that music, like all of the arts, exists for human beings, that it has its origins in human needs and human impulses. If criteria are to be valid, they must be ultimately relevant to this fact. It is quite true that, in our day, various forces—political in some cases, commercial in others—have misused this principle in the service of ends diametrically opposed to its real meaning. But the ultimate human relevance of music, as of art in general, has to do with the level on which it operates, not with its immediate acceptance by a large public. It is after all the depth, the intensity, and the persistence of the response that a work evokes which determines its ultimate destiny, and not the numerical statistics of the applause that it receives at any given moment.

What I have written in the preceding paragraphs bears only in part on the enormous volume of aesthetic controversy that abounds in the artistic world today. Certainly it is clear that a proportion of this, too, is the result of competitive maneuvering, and has little substance apart from it. I heard, some years ago, of a European promoter who made a specialty of concocting arresting quasi-artistic slogans for groups of artists desiring to capture the limelight by such means. Given all we know of contemporary life and publicity, it would be surprising if things of this kind did not occur fairly frequently.

However, the fact that this is so has no bearing whatever on the fact that the aesthetic turmoil of today is quite genuine and that many gifted and serious musicians, like artists in other fields, are genuinely impelled to explore new regions of sensibility, and that it is through the persistence of such impulses that the arts continue to develop and hence to exist. One is not entitled to dismiss the results simply because one's eyebrows rise at some of the claims made for them. All I am saying, after all, is that a willing ear must not only be genuinely willing, but must function as a genuine ear. If what we call the arts are to survive it will be, at least in large part, because human beings do not lose or abandon their ability to respond, directly and without constraint or prejudice, to whatever life has to offer them, regardless of the way in which the goods are packaged; regardless also of the pressures to ignore and distrust one's own instincts, to which everyone is to some degree subjected by the market, by established institutions, by the "academy," by fashion and publicity. We all know about these pressures, and ignore or yield to them in accordance with the degree and authenticity of our cultural involvement. In the final analysis, criteria are no more or less than the means by which we preserve what we want, and discard or let go what we do not. Thus their very existence is a condition not only of the vitality of the arts, but of human liberty in any sense that is real.

What, finally, does the willing ear hope to find in music? Barring lengthy and, in the end, inconclusive discussion one can answer this question verbally only in the most general terms, and I shall try to sketch some partial indications. Let us take *craft* for granted, since it is only as a result of craft that anything is present at all; craft should be counted as a necessary premise, not a quality. First of all, I would be tempted to say, the willing ear hopes to find *novelty*. In other words, we do not wish to hear music that is essentially a repetition of something that we have heard before. But perhaps novelty is not quite the right word; there is novelty on a great many different levels, beginning on the level where what is new ceases to be so after we have heard it once or at most a very few times. There is also, incidentally, a fairly rare type of novelty which begins to appear only when we know the music fairly well. Let us adopt another image, not that of novelty but that of *character;* music must have a *face of its own.* This also is not invariably recognizable at first glance; most of us are familiar with the saying that "all Chinese look alike"—a statement well designed to illustrate the hazards of premature categorization. In other words, when objects—or styles—are unfamiliar, we may easily be so aware of the fact of unfamiliarity which they have in common that we overlook the very palpable differences that begin to appear as soon as the initial shock of unfamiliarity has worn off. It is these differences, however, which are crucial. Music must indeed have a face, an identity; a work of art aims eventually not at novelty as such, but at uniqueness.

In the service of this aim, it needs the quality of *boldness.* I have often proposed to my students Danton's motto: *De l'audace, toujours de l'audace, et encore de l'audace!* This means, of course, genuine boldness: boldness both in conception and execution, in style and where necessary in vocabulary and technique. The music's gestures, in other words, must be decisive and unequivocal, and completely secure in their aim. All this is what boldness means; it does not mean simply unconventionality, which can very quickly and easily become quite conventional if not motivated by a genuine and fresh musical impulse. The trouble with "novelty" pursued for its own sake is that, if this impulse is not behind it, it quickly degenerates into cliché—and this is a problem with which every generation of younger composers, including the present one, has to cope. Boldness implies indifference to convention, not merely a stereotyped revolt against it; and it implies a novelty of substance, not merely of gadgetry or technical procedure.

I can think of three more words implying criteria that seem to me important. I have just used the term *substance*. I would describe substance very roughly as that which remains when the initial novelty has worn off. It implies, certainly, character, and character that is manifest not only in the face but, so to speak, in the bones and the bloodstream of the music. In other words, something must really happen in the music, something that retains our interest and assumes, and eventually retains, significance for us.

Of course, substance is in the last analysis inextricably bound up with design, the musical nature of which I discussed in the previous chapter. Since I am not here concerned with definitions, I do not wish to belabor a distinction between design and substance. It would in any case involve simply the age-old discussion of form and content all over again. I have always been convinced that, properly understood, the two—form and content—are identical. But recognizing this identity involves acknowledgment of the fact that design which is merely abstract, which is not conceived in terms of concrete musical ideas and musical gesture, is not musical design at all but a contrived imitation thereof. Substance, in these terms, is not merely a prerequisite of genuine design, but of its very essence.

I mentioned three words, of which *substance* was only the first. The other two are *consistency* and *inevitability*. Both denote essential but elusive characteristics of a musical work; they are in fact so elusive that I was tempted to leave them out altogether, since my survey is a designedly cursory one. I introduce them for very brief comment, in order to point out some common pitfalls that are frequently apparent in their current mode of usage. "Consistency" or, as it is often called, "unity of style," is indeed an essential element in music. The problem in applying it as a criterion is simply that of discovering in what the "style" or character really consists, in each given instance. I have on occasion been told that *Die Zauber-flöte* (*The Magic Flute*) is "an impossible mixture of styles" —a very strange comment, it seems to me, on a mature work by Wolfgang Amadeus Mozart. One must be sure of one's categories—sure, that is, that they are real in terms of music itself, and not in terms of a filing system that one has found convenient for the purposes of, let us say, pedagogy, historiography, journalism, or, indeed, for any purpose whatever.

As for "inevitability," I believe this too is an important musical criterion, not unconnected with what I have tried to describe as consistency. First of all, artistically speaking, what we call the "inevitable" should not be confused with what we mean by the term "obvious." The latter term denotes a flagging of creative energy, the former should denote its undiverted continuity. One must never forget that what we call inevitability is the result of a clear and totally realized conception of the composer, and not simply a result of either technical dexterity or a kind of determinism based on the initial musical idea of the composer himself. It is the end product, in other words, of *choices* that the composer makes, and constantly, in the course of his work, and the nature of the choices will be determined by his conception, either in the making or in the process of realization.

The contrary of the *inevitable* is the *contrived*. We find a passage, or a work, or a style contrived when we become more aware of the processes by which it is made than of the musical substance itself. Since I am speaking here in generalities, I shall not attempt to enumerate the various—and varied—factors that may contribute to such a result. Obviously, technical procedures that engage our attention only as such, and not as essential elements in a convincing musical design, will impress us as irrelevant, and if we choose to consider the matter fully, as inept, even on a specifically technical level.

There are other words I could discuss, of course. *Sincerity?* It is a term of very doubtful applicability to works of the imagination. Insofar as it makes any sense at all, it is amply and far more effectively covered in terms of the criteria I have already discussed. *Clarity,* of course, and also *simplicity*—but these are possible as criteria only within the framework of specific contexts. One cannot regard them as valid criteria otherwise than in terms of the utmost clarity and simplicity possible within a given conception. On these terms they are vital criteria indeed.

No discussion of criteria can be quite complete or even, perhaps, quite valid unless it indicates on the part of the author some awareness of the music that is most controversial at the time the discussion takes place, and some indication of the author's personal basis of judgment regarding that music. For that reason I shall comment briefly on the music of the younger generation of today. I have already indicated my basic attitude toward it. As Gustav Mahler said—and, I believe, in the sense that I interpreted his remark—"The younger generation is always right." I shall not repeat my interpretation here; I will, however, add that, well before the advent of the present "avant-garde," I had learned to remain unimpressed—and therefore undismayed—by slogans; I have heard too many of them, and learned to understand both their function and their limited applicability as far as musical results are concerned.

I have listened attentively to very much music of what is called the avant-garde, and have had varying reactions to it. This does not include the reaction of "shock," which at my age I would have expected. The greatest shock of that kind I have ever felt—and by "shock" I do not mean a necessarily disagreeable, but rather a dramatic experience—came during my sophomore year at Harvard, when at the age of fifteen I was confronted with the music of Arnold Schönberg for the first time. It is many years since I have heard any music that has seemed to me difficult to anything like the same degree. I am not sure that I wholly understand the reasons why this has been so. It is partly, of course, that my own ear has developed since that time, through many years of listening, and above all, composing; it is also, I suspect, because the doors which Schönberg and his contemporaries opened led to regions that are still being explored, and that must be far more fully explored and cultivated, and assimilated, before another and equally challenging set of doors is encountered.

I do not, therefore, consider that I am in any way or to any degree belittling the music of the most recent years in saying that I do not find any of it enormously "difficult to listen to." I have heard music by younger composers that I have disliked, but I have never had the impression that my dislike had much to do with the question of whether the music was "far out" or not; sometimes it was, but at least as often not particularly so. I have heard music that was equally "far out"—insofar as one can measure such things—and been genuinely impressed by it. My only conclusion would be that I am always interested in what music *is,* and not in the least in what it is not; and sometimes "distance out" is more negative in intent—which is very easy—than positive. It seems more preoccupied, that is to say, with qualities or characteristics that the composer wishes—sometimes rather desperately —to avoid than with a positive and genuinely affirmative conception. On the other hand, some music that is very "far out" indeed has impressed me as showing very considerable talent and possessing genuine character. I have heard many a concert or even concert-series of so-called "avant-garde" music which has impressed me as a succession of strings of clichés fashionable at the particular moment. But every now and then something has stood out because of having seemed to me to take real shape; it has struck me by its definiteness and its differences from everything else on the program.

In order to make clear a point which I consider of capital importance: I have been genuinely impressed by music that was to a large extent aleatoric, and have even defended it warmly on occasion. I have also been impressed by music that embodied principles of "total serialization." I have certainly been bored by music of both kinds, and neither of these two ideas—so-called "chance music" and total serialism—seems to me to have any validity as a general principle. But the point I am making is that a composer of authentic talent and imagination, and of course craft, will somehow succeed in achieving results that are genuinely musical, with everything he seriously uses—sometimes almost in spite of himself. He accomplishes this not by dint of effort, but because he cannot do otherwise—because this is the natural shape which his ideas will take. Clearly this does not mean that all the music that he produces will be of equal value—that after all has never been true of anyone. It will not necessarily be of any real value whatever. But it will be something that really takes shape, even if only on the most modest level. This is only the beginning, perhaps merely the premise, of artistic achievement. In like manner, it is our awareness of the distinction here implied which furnishes us with the touchstone that must form the basis—and the premise—upon which criteria are developed, and without which even the concept of criteria would remain without meaning.

Epilogue

I SUPPOSE IT IS CLEAR from all that I have written thus far that I am not discouraged in regard to the state of music today. Such a statement, however, requires considerable elucidation if, in a time like ours, it is to make any sense whatever. Not only are the pessimistic forecasts that one constantly hears too insistent and too widespread to be totally ignored, but the facts themselves, as anyone strongly involved with the cultural world observes them each day, are such as to give one constant and ample grounds for concern.

That which prompts my lack of discouragement is my conviction that gifted young people are as anxious as they ever were to create music, and that those whom I consider gifted are neither, in my judgment, discernibly less gifted nor fewer in number, or less serious in their aims, than those I have known in previous generations. Such comparisons are frequently made, of course, and on the flimsiest of bases; and our modern tendency to think in journalistic terms inclines us not only to the habit of constantly taking our cultural temperature, as it were, at hourly intervals, but also to incessant "interpretation," as we are wont to call our more or less clever, and often not wholly disinterested, guessing. We indulge in this pastime often in a quite facile manner, without allowing ourselves to remain too much aware of the multitude of intangibles involved—intangibles clearly inherent not only in the observable facts, but in the predilections, the temperament, and the basic interests and intellectual attitudes of the observer. My own judgment, of course, is as subject to these qualifications as is that of anyone else, and I can say in its support only that it is based on considerable experience, and has been arrived at as conscientiously as possible. It involves what I know of the personal resources, in terms of musical ability, inventiveness, involvement, vitality of sense and feeling, and genuine independence, that I have observed in numerous young musicians, both composers and performers. I have on various occasions felt compelled to recognize these qualities, as it were, in the face of slogans which seemed to me irrelevant and even at times nonsensical. "So what!" one must sometimes say, but then one is still obliged to apply one's query in both directions. If the slogans are irrelevant, then one must look beyond them not only for the possibility that the product may well be fraudulent, but also for the possibility that it may be of interest and even of value. It sometimes is. The decisive question is: what does the slogan really mean to the composer himself? Conceivably it may be a point of departure, a genuine spur to his imagination. It may be, and very frequently is, a badge of conformity—a party button—or on a considerably higher level, it may be a token of identity adopted basically for self-protection, in order to mitigate the palpable discomforts that, today probably even more than in the past, constitute the price which is exacted for genuine independence and integrity.

The only matter of importance is the musical result; and I am convinced that music of genuine force and substance, of real independence and of human import, is being created by young composers on both sides of the Atlantic, in all four quarters of the globe, and on both sides of the Iron Curtain. The fact that a far larger amount of music written today has little real interest, that its failings or shortcomings can be diagnosed under a variety of headings, ranging from the academic to the fraudulent, is not in any sense peculiar to our time. It has always been so; but the inferior music of the past has for the most part disappeared, and we tend to forget or ignore the fact that it ever existed.

What *is* peculiar to our time is the enormous proliferation of publicity, much of it expressly designed to confuse judgment. It would be sheer nonsense to underestimate the effect of this; but we can, and should, recognize that it has no more to do with the real facts of the situation than have had similar manifestations at any previous time. Its danger today derives from its enormous and ubiquitous quantity, its perfected techniques, and its befuddling effect upon the body politic. A more precise statement, of course, would emphasize the uses to which this highly developed technique is put—the very prevalent practice, among public figures, of thinking in terms of "images" that may or may not have any very clear relationship to either character or accomplishment; or the constant flow of propaganda from official sources and the "credibility gap" that must inevitably result, since, after all, we as human beings are not only trained to use our minds, but compelled to do so in most of the exigencies of our daily lives.

Such matters are not, of course, the subject of the present volume; but they are one tangible element in the inevitable point of arrival which is implicit in any serious discussion of the prospects faced by music, the arts, or culture in general. It should be clear that all such questions are simply aspects of the far more serious, and increasingly urgent, question of human survival—whether we are to allow ourselves to be blown to the four winds, or eaten away by radiation, in a nuclear orgy; or to starve to death through overpopulation; or to experience a slow, or perhaps not so slow, disintegration through the increasing pollution of our natural environment; or, perhaps most menacing because least perceptible of all, whether we will gradually allow our basic human liberties to be eroded in the pursuit of comfort and a chimerical "security," in the name of social organization, to the point where we find ourselves engulfed in the morass of a technological utopia in which men and women will have to all intents and purposes become automata, and the least sign of individuality, on any level whatever, will come finally to be regarded as a danger, to be decisively extirpated. Let me say, as I have repeatedly implied, that I do not regard any of these developments as inevitable. But anyone who looks at the human situation seriously must be aware that there are very powerful forces at large—including certain "traditional" modes of thought— which are pushing constantly in each of these directions; there is also a widely diffused tendency to ignore, to mini-mize, or even to accept these forces, resignedly or com-placently, in the name of "historical necessity," "fate," "realism," or whatever deterministic slogan seems appropriate at the moment. This has always been the totalitarian thrust, and constitutes its ultimate horror, which has sometimes been partially obscured by the more immediate and more dramatic horror of its more spectacular manifestations. Those who look at the facts squarely are often stigmatized as "prophets of doom," though what they actually are doing is calling atten-tion to stubborn facts that must be faced sooner or later, and the consequences which must follow with virtual certainty if they are not faced in time.

The future of the arts, obviously, depends on these matters of urgent human import, and to a far greater extent than it does upon the trends or fashions (or "styles") that happen to be in vogue at any given moment. As far as these latter are concerned, it is easy to see that they are infinitely more complex and far less monolithic than many of us would find it convenient to think. As I have already indicated, the same apparent trend may be, and often is, in reality composed of both negative and positive elements—the desire simply to repudiate "the past" and the genuine impulse to create something new. Since the past is often "repudiated" by people who have little idea in what the "past" really consisted, the picture becomes often a bizarre, confused, and thoroughly trivial one, and we find ourselves confronted with a play on "images" that have little valid substance, and that evoke only a kind of symbolic interest, having little or nothing to do with the actual musical object, in and for itself. Instead of music, as such, by any viable definition, embodied in works of genuine substance and clear profile, we find ourselves often confronted by "kinds of music" in which the piece itself is of little or no significance; it is the trend or slogan that furnishes an easy ideological standard of evaluation, which is quite independent of the artistic object as such. Obviously, a trend has no real existence except in terms of works that have considerably more to offer than the mere and decidedly tenuous excitement provided by the fact of representing a "trend." But this seems all too often to be forgotten or ignored.

Trends do exist, of course; those that really matter, however, are the ones which are relevant to a much larger framework. The framework is at least as often as not far from clearly envisaged by the promoters of the specific trend. But it should be clear that artistic movements, on any scale, derive their substance and their value from significant works, which create and embody them—not the reverse.

All of this actually belongs among the manifestations of what contemporary parlance refers to as "mass culture." Unfortunately, the latter term has in practice acquired a number of different meanings, some of which are at variance with the clear meaning of the word "culture" itself. In its original sense it refers to the principle, not only laudable but essential, that the cultural resources belong to the people as a whole, and should be made abundantly available to everyone who desires them. In practice, however, it has frequently become a slogan heralding the development of vast new fields for commercial enterprise. This very patent fact can scarcely be said to have simplified the cultural picture, or to have contributed to its clarification; and much of the confusion with which we are today all too familiar can easily be traced to its multiple and often very subtle ramifications. I referred briefly in my opening chapter to the ineluctable and virtually automatic drive of any commercial field toward expansion, thus toward winning a continually larger consuming public. The inevitable and indeed the only possible result of this drive— and this is of fateful significance where the arts are concerned —is that the wares, offered by enterprises which are dependent upon profits, are geared to the less involved elements of the public, not to those who, because of their initial and strong involvement, may presumably be taken for granted as customers. There is always the risk of alienating the latter, of course, and there are some signs that this is actually happening, perhaps to an increasing degree. The process nevertheless goes on, with the tendency to shift the emphasis gradually from that which demands, and generates, strong and continuing involvement to that which is merely entertaining or, to a lesser extent, that which for any reason, not necessarily connected with music, is capable of producing a "sensation" of one kind or another—provided always that the "sensation" be obvious enough to demand no particular effort on the part of the public. I have stated the matter rather crassly, of course. Certainly the situation to which I am referring derives in part not merely from what I have called "commercial enterprise" in the raw, but also from such facts as that, for instance, a considerable number of our musical institutions that formerly enjoyed security through private patronage have for many years— roughly since the end of the First World War—been unable to do so, and have been obliged in some measure to seek profits in order to remain in existence. The struggle is a hard one, and involves ineluctably the adoption, to a very considerable extent, of the commercial, or if you prefer, "business," point of view.

I am not complaining about this situation, or condemning those involved in it; nor am I suggesting that the problems could have been solved by other means. The blunt, but fundamental fact of the matter is that the "performing" arts have never to any real extent been self-supporting, and cannot exist for very long in a healthy condition if they are to be continually subject to the demands—and the vicissitudes— of the market.

From the standpoint of the arts themselves the most crucial fact at this particular moment is the process involved in "selling" them to an ever-expanding public, or, in economic terms, a growing body of consumers. A by-product of that process is the gradual transference of values from those proper to the art itself to those inherent in, and therefore fostered by, the selling process. Certainly the term "selling process" implies an oversimplification of the actual facts of the matter. But the infiltration of economic interests, sometimes large-scale ones, into strictly musical matters tends to give new and artistically irrelevant meanings to concepts proper to the general category of artistic worth. Thus the idea of "popularity," which would seem to imply some degree of genuine involvement, tends to be transmuted into the principle of salability, an essentially short-range commercial matter that implies no necessity of real involvement whatever. As we all have plenty of opportunity to observe, the most immediately salable goods are not necessarily the most permanently satisfying ones. This is clearly evident, and generally accepted, in regard to the past. As I tried to point out in my first chapter, many of the greatest masterpieces which have survived and are still "doing well" have never become "popular" in any very literal sense.

The past, in fact, is generally regarded as essentially immune, and unproblematical. At the very least, it is manageable and, as we say, "accepted." Paradoxically, there is a hidden danger in this, too; and its symptoms have already begun to appear in quite definite form, from various directions. If such a tendency should persist and continue developing, it would certainly mean that our relation to the music of former periods would quickly become quite static, and lose the vitality which it has thus far possessed for us. Not only would opinion regarding it become frozen—which is to say dead—but we would cease to expect, or to seek, in the music of the present, qualities of experience and satisfaction comparable in intensity or in significance to those which lovers of music have always sought and found in music, past or present. The tendency in question would, in other words, eventually result in a break in continuity forced upon the arts by circumstances, and having little to do with the arts or the human spirit that they embody, a break radically different in nature from that embodied in the phrase "off with the old, on with the new," which is the legitimate watchword of each generation which comes up with authentically fresh ideas of its own. I am quite aware that there are those who, for a rather bizarre variety of reasons, and with a somewhat less bizarre variety of reactions, would have it that this has already taken place or—abetted by the weary and lazy, though all too fashionable determinism to which I have already referred— that it is "inevitable."

I can only repeat my conviction, for which I have already given my reasons, that this is not so; that our institutional "set-up" may well and almost certainly will change, but that music itself is still in a fundamentally healthy state. This is not at all to say that we are in the midst, or on the threshold, of a period of florescence comparable to the greatest ones of the past. Though questions of this kind are sometimes raised, they seem to me quite beside the point, for reasons that I have at least adumbrated in the preceding chapters. Though, in the course of sixty years' intense involvement with music and musical life, I have lived through times that seemed to me intensely exciting in terms of general musical production and activity, I have never imagined that such times were quite like musical Vienna in the eighteenth and early nineteenth centuries, the Elizabethan period in England, the *Grand Siècle* in France, or the Renaissance in Italy. Of course no one alive in my lifetime has had a really precise idea of how those periods seemed, in terms of actual experience, to their contemporaries. A writer who identifies himself as a determined pallbearer of so-called "serious music" today has made much of the fact that while Beethoven's funeral, in 1827, was attended by high dignitaries and participated in by the most famed vocal celebrities of the day, no such pomp was forthcoming for Schönberg's, in 1951. He might, of course, investigate the details of Mozart's funeral—also in Vienna, and at the height of the great Viennese period, in 1791. His palpably crude statement would decidedly not be worth quoting here if it did not illustrate the lengths to which a fairly prevalent pseudo-historicism can be carried on occasion. What is so often forgotten is that, merely because music must be kept alive to an overwhelming degree through performance, and because much music even of considerable merit therefore often disappears rather quickly from view after a period of popularity, our idea of even the greatest historical periods is inevitably distorted. Not only do we take Haydn, Mozart, Beethoven, and Schubert for granted as—with the possible exception of Haydn in his later years—their contemporaries never quite succeeded in doing; but we have entirely lost sight of the great mass of their confrères who filled the bulk of the programs of that day, and some of whom then enjoyed an esteem and a popularity at least comparable to that of the four who have so triumphantly survived. At the same time the latter remained, in varying degrees, "controversial." As far as lifetime success-stories go, Haydn could be fairly well matched by Stravinsky, Beethoven by Schönberg (with allowances, of course, for the former's patronage from sources of a kind and status that have for a very long time simply ceased to exist, and also for the latter's ultimate condition as a refugee), and Mozart and Schubert by Bartók and Berg and Webern. The most palpable differences could be easily traced to the enormous social, political, geographical, and economic differences of the two periods, and could be argued back and forth indefinitely on that basis. The names I have mentioned are not those of the present generation, of course; but it is the period initiated by them that is under attack, and we can see them in some perspective. My only point is that such considerations have exactly nothing to do with ultimate value, one way or the other. Once again, and for the last time in this book, it is only the music, and its final impact on those who learn to know and respond to it, that counts.

So, I must end my discussion on a note of duly qualified non-discouragement, and the firm conviction that the future of music—and all of the other arts—rests not only or even primarily on the artists themselves, but to an overwhelming degree on the future of mankind. It seems to me essentially frivolous to speculate on the future of the arts in any other terms. Do we wish them to sink into the role of "bread and circuses," or not? Should this take place, however, it would be only a by-product of a much larger and more fateful human development; to no degree could it be considered an independent phenomenon.

I am not in any sense implying that artists have no responsibilities, or that whatever failings they may possess, as artists or otherwise, are to be passed over to that abstract and sometimes rather vague monster which we call "society." Perhaps, in fact, we should shift some of our interest from "society" to the needs, impulses, and even the dreams of human beings, not as puppets, cogs in the machine, or statistics—or "casualties," actual or potential—but as fellow creatures with instincts and desires, minds and problems, like the rest of us.

As do all dedicated people, artists possess very specific

responsibilities, of the nature of which I hope I have given some clear indication in the preceding pages: responsibilities of craftsmanship, of singlemindedness, and to the limits of their capabilities, of vision and imagination. Other responsibilities they share with the rest of mankind, and obviously the specifically artistic responsibilities must be considered an integral part of these. This of course does not imply conformity, which, to quote once more my late friend Ben Shahn, is "a failure of hope or belief or rebellion." He adds: "Non-conformity is the basic pre-condition of art, as it is the pre-condition of good thinking and therefore of growth and greatness in a people."[1] I could not agree more, nor could I imagine a better way of stating the fact. What the human responsibility of the artist means is above all awareness of the human condition, a common involvement and a common stake in it. I believe the most promising younger musicians of today realize all of this as fully as their predecessors always have done, and it is in this conviction that I dedicate this book to them—with no strings attached!

[1] Ben Shahn, *The Shape of Content* (Cambridge, Mass.: Harvard University Press, 1957), p. 87.